THE
ROLLER
CANARY

GW01057430

REVISED BY GEORGE PRESKEY
FROM THE ORIGINAL BY H W GUTIERREZ
Published in conjunction with **The British Roller Canary Association**

ii

THE ROLLER CANARY

By H.W. Gutierrez
Revised by George Preskey

Beech Publishing House
15 The Maltings,
Turk St
Alton
Hants GU34 1DL

Beech Publishing House
15 The Maltings,
Turk St
Alton
Hants GU34 1DL

Roller Canary in Full Song

CONTENTS

· THE ROLLER FANCY TODAY

TWO organisations currently govern the affairs of the Roller Fancy. Broadly speaking clubs in the North of England are affiliated to The British Roller Canary Association (B.R.C.A.) and clubs in the Midlands and South to The National Roller Canary Society (N.R.C.S.).

There is close co-operation between the two organisations, which apply virtually identical rules to the contesting of birds and share the same panel of judges. Weekly open singing contests are held between November and March, alternating between the two. All roller judges must be experienced fanciers, who have passed a stringent theoretical and practical examination and must be currently active as breeders and exhibitors.

All contest birds must wear the official closed ring and ring numbers of winning birds are published in the show catalogue. All exhibitors, whether successful or not are provided with a points sheet after the show showing the points awarded to each of their birds for the tours they have sung.

The current range of tours and maximum points allowed is:

Hollow Roll	11
Bass	11
Water Gluck	10
Gluck	10
Gluck Roll	10
Hollow Bell	8
Schockel	8
Flutes	6
Water Roll	6
Deep Bubbling Water Tour	5
Bell Roll	3
Bell Tour	2
General Effect	10
TOTAL	100

Maximum points to be deducted for faults:

Faulty Gluck	6
Faulty Flutes	6
Hard Aufzug	3
Bad Nasal Tour	6
Faulty Bells	6
Ugly Interjections	6

THE ROLLER CANARY

CHAPTER I

INTRODUCTION

BEFORE the first edition of " The Roller Canary " appeared there was little written in these islands expounding the song or dealing with the training of the Roller Canary. Time has emphasized the need of a text book within reach of all lovers of the British Roller Canary, and which, if they are blessed with a musical ear, will enable them not only to breed and rear these lovely songsters, but will educate them in the multiplicity of his tours and their variations and thus place them in a position to appreciate in full the excellent and good, as well as to condemn the unworthy and the bad.

In the case of a novice, the help and guidance gained from his fellow breeders who are familiar with the tours will profitably and effectually be supplemented by what he finds here, and if, in the light of the explanations and definitions given him in this work, he studies his own birds at home and those of others he may come across, it will be a frequent source of interest and pleasure to him.

" The Roller Canary " is based upon experiences of both English and foreign breeders, and I have no hesitation in saying it is authoritative. Tastes differ; experts differ, and many experts may not agree with all that is laid down here. I venture to hope that it will prove useful and educative and interesting to all.

The reader is asked to pardon the use of foreign words, and foreign vowels. As regards the former, most of them are manufactured in imitation of the notes of the birds. As regards the vowels, it is common knowledge that our five English vowels do not represent all the vowel sounds, such for instance as the French or Welsh " u," the Italian " o," etc. I have therefore set forth a short simple list of vowel signs and their English equivalents, and the reader will find it easy to familiarize himself with them.

Vowels used in this treatise and their English equivalents :

a is pronounced as a in papa, haha.

e is pronounced as our short a in mate, rate.

i is pronounced as e in fee, glee.

o is pronounced as o in go, no.

u is pronounced as oo in pool, cool.

ä is pronounced as our long a in hay, way.

ö is pronounced as u in fur, cur, without rolling the "r."

ü is the French or Welsh u; it is pronounced as ee (fee) with the lips rounded, and almost closed, as in whistling ; the sound is half-way between our " u " and "e."

The reader should pay particular attention to the pronunciation of the vowels used in describing the song, as this crucial definition has frequently been omitted in other theses, leading to serious misunderstanding

CHAPTER II

SELECTION OF BREEDING STOCK

A GOOD start is everything in a race or a battle, even so in the breeding of Roller Canaries. There are two or three points we would impress most forcibly upon our readers. The first is to start with birds of one strain, the second to have none but thoroughly healthy birds, and the third is to select the breeding stock and let it be in the breeding room as soon after the finish of the moult in the autumn as it is possible.

The reasons why? The man who has a successful strain of birds has made it by continued and persistent selection over many years, so that you are, in buying stock from such a man, buying the results of his skill and experience. When birds of varied strains are mated together the result is never, or hardly ever, satisfactory, because the blood does not hit. Then health. Birds that are not healthy are useless as breeders as they produce nothing but weak, delicate progeny that is of little use. Thirdly, when birds are placed in the room in which they are to be mated in the autumn and live in it all through the winter they become accustomed to the surroundings, their food, and their attendants, and the results are infinitely better than when they are only introduced to the breeding room just previous to being mated up. This applies more particularly to hens than cocks.

Those who reside in London, Manchester, Bolton, Leeds and other large towns have a great advantage over those who live in country districts, as they are able to join one or other of the Roller Canary Clubs and by associating with the members learn much as to the value of birds and where the best are to be found. Those not so situated are dependent on the reports of contests which appear in "Cage Birds," and the advertisement pages of that journal.

BUY FROM THE BEST STRAINS.

In making a start the novice who is without previous experience of the Roller Canary should secure birds from a first-class strain, but he should not buy the best, that is, competition stock, as because of his lack of knowledge and experience he may quickly reap much disappointment and waste a lot of money.

For the first season or two it is wise to go slow so as to learn not only how to breed and rear the young properly, but also to gain all the knowledge possible as to the song. Knowledge it takes years to acquire.

We have said the stock should be purchased in the autumn, especially the hens. It is not always possible to buy young cocks from a good strain in the early autumn, as many breeders will not sell young cocks until they have tried them out, and tested their song. It is, however, possible to purchase young hens, and yearling or two year old cocks, and the best results are likely to result from the breeding of youth and age. It is not wise to breed from first season birds only. Experience teaches that the best results are achieved when there is age on one side or the other.

THE TOWNSMAN'S ADVANTAGE

We have spoken of the advantages possessed by those who live in towns and cities where Roller Canary Clubs are in existence; introductions and recommendations to noted breeders are easily obtained through the officials of such clubs. The best men in these clubs are always ready and willing to do what they can to help a new beginner. Whether you buy from someone to whom you have had a personal introduction, or from someone whose advertisements have caught your eye, it is wise to place yourself unreservedly in their hands. Tell them exactly what money you can afford to spend, and also what you are desirous of accomplishing. If you are hoping to join the ranks of exhibitors, or if you are only about to indulge in the breeding of Roller Canaries as a hobby without any idea of entering competitions it is wise to let the persons from whom you are buying know just what your ambition is. There are few old fanciers who will take advantage of a novice, that is if he places himself unreservedly in their hands.

BUYING FROM STRANGERS

Although we advise the beginner not to purchase first-class birds at the start yet we just as emphatically urge upon him the importance of purchasing his initial stock from a first-class strain. By so doing he may possibly breed a champion right away, and even if he does not, the young birds which he does breed will sell far better, because of their pedigree, than would birds that were mere songsters.

Those who are not able to secure an introduction to a high-class breeder should study well the competition reports in " Cage Birds," select a breeder who has been successful and write to him, stating their requirements, and at the same time asking him for prices and particulars of birds he may have to sell.

Those who are experienced can select hens equally as well as they can select cocks. They can detect music in the call note. Depth of song is of the greatest importance, and those who are experienced select those hens for breeding which possess a deep, mellow call note.

The advantage of going to a good man, that is a breeder of experience, is that you are buying pedigree and all it carries with it in stamina and song. Stamina is essential, not only because of what it does in the way of power of song, but also because birds from a strain noted for stamina are generally good breeders and good feeders. That is, they are prolific, and tend their young well. Sickly, weakly, delicate birds are of no use to anyone. They are an unending source of annoyance and disappointment. Therefore, do we say--that in all your buying see to it that you buy healthy stock.

Birds that are healthy are bright and full in the eye, their plumage lies close and compactly, they are brisk in their movements, their notes are clear and distinct, and their excreta is firm and of a natural colour. Avoid birds who pass excreta that is greenish in colour, and slimy in texture.

BREEDING FROM TUTORS

One is often asked if it is advisable to use a tutor for breeding, and if the same would spoil the song. If a tutor can be kept without being mated in his first year, then it is always advisable to do so. Widely different methods are necessary in the case of a tutor and a stock male bird. The former is to be kept in pure song, with the ultimate object of being used to transmit this song to the young birds. While on the stock bird we depend for the correct fertilization of all eggs laid by the hens to which he will be mated.

To keep the tutor in low and faultless song, it is necessary that the bird should be kept in a cabinet, with restricted light, and a nourishing, but not too stimulating diet. With the stock male, the reverse is the case. To be successful in obtaining fertile eggs, the male bird must be vigorous and strong. He must be given plenty of exercise, and at the proper time the diet must be both rich and stimulating. This must be kept up all the way through the breeding season, otherwise the first nest may be good, but the second and third not so satisfactory. The fact that stock birds are too closely confined immediately prior to pairing to their respective hens is responsible for many failures. Stock males should be given all the exercise possible, and if a large aviary is not available then the birds should be placed in a large flight cage for some time before mating. Fanciers will have to be prepared to sacrifice a little in song in order to obtain this required condition.

CHAPTER III

THE BREEDING SEASON

WHEN "The Roller Canary" was first written the great majority of canaries were bred in an attic or spare room in the dwelling house, in relatively warm conditions and breeding could start by pairing in March. When breeding in outside birdrooms, as is more usual today, it is wiser to delay the pairing of the birds until the first few weeks in April, but in any case pairing should not take place until the birds show all the signs of being ready. This will vary according to geographical location and whether artificial heat and light have been used. Most modern fanciers now plan to take only two nests.

KEEP STRANGERS AWAY

When canaries are breeding many seem to be very nervous and excitable, and while they are not upset by the presence of one who usually takes care of them, they are quick to notice strangers, and will stop the work in which they are engaged during their presence. This is especially noticeable at the time when hens are feeding young birds. A good rule is to prevent if possible persons going into the breeding room while the birds are nesting. When birds are used to strangers no ill effects arise. Some fanciers have visitors in their rooms every week, and the birds are used to strangers, thus no harm is done, but when birds are not used to strange voices at ordinary times they should not be allowed to be disturbed during the breeding season.

NEVER BREED LATE

It is a great temptation when one has had a bad breeding season to take "just one more nest," so as to level things up. More often than not it levels them down. The early bad luck has possibly been due to the fact that one or other of the parent birds has not been in first-class condition, and to take a further nest of eggs from them would mean a further tax on an enfeebled and delicate body. Good, or bad, though the season be—never breed late.

Many of the troubles which afflict the Canary breeder are due to late breeding. Late-bred birds never moult properly, the season is against them, and late breeding retards the moult of the old birds. A slow moult, or a retarded moult, is never a healthy moult, and the evil consequences of such are sure to be manifest in the next breeding season. It means impaired health and vitality in the stock.

THE BREEDING CAGES

There is a great difference in the ways in which fanciers conduct their breeding operations. Some use small flights into which they turn six or eight hens and a couple of cocks, others run two or three hens with one cock in a large flight cage, and others run two hens with a cock in what are known as double-compartment breeding cages, whilst others, whether they run a cock with one, two, or three hens let each hen have a separate cage, running the cock with each hen in rotation. We do not care for this system. The best results come from individual pairs, and never would we run more than two hens with a cock. If one desires to keep up the vigour and stamina of the stock one cock to one hen is the best way to secure that end.

FITTING THE CAGES

The cages may be hung on the wall, or stacked in frames, but when stacked they should not touch each other, and never should they touch the wall. Keep them away from the wall and stack by small screws, and thus avoid breeding grounds for red mite.

The cage should be 20 ins. long, 11 ins. deep from front to back, and 18 ins. high. The nest pan should be fixed at the back, being hung on a screw, and at such a height that the old birds may feed the young easily whilst standing on the perch which runs from front to back. The cage should have two such perches fixed about 4 ins. from the end of the cage. The seed and drinking vessels should be fixed on the outside of the cage, and there should be a couple of egg drawers, either in the front woodwork or else in the wirework. One of these can be used for egg food or its substitute, and one for tit-bits in the way of special seeds.

SAND OR SAWDUST

Never neglect the provision of a bath pan. Let your birds bathe every other day. It will keep them healthy and keep down insect life.

B

There is division of opinion on the use of sand or sawdust on the floor of the cage. We prefer the former. Sawdust gets in the food and on the top of the water, and as it is not digestible does a great deal of harm to the young birds. Clean the cages out twice a week, scatter a fair covering of fine gritty sand on the bottom, and we believe you will meet with more success than if you adopt the other system of sawdust on the floor and sand in a tin or tray. Often the latter is forgotten, and grit is as essential to the welfare of birds as is food. Wash the perches every week. Remember that cleanliness is a great aid to success. The cages should be thoroughly cleansed before the birds are mated up.

•

LET THEM BE FIT

When the birds are paired they should both be thoroughly fit. Never pair birds unless they are full of life, vivacity, and movement. When birds are quiet and listless in their movements they are not fit to undertake the task of bringing other birds into the world. As pairing time approaches—long days and mild weather —the hens that are fit will be hopping and flying about the cages carrying pieces of fluff, strong feathers, or other light material that may find its way into the cages. They will be quick and active in their movements, standing on the perches flapping their wings and calling to the cocks. When these signs are observed in a hen, you may justly conclude she is ready for mating. But be sure all these signs are present. The cocks are generally ready before the hens. But be sure they are ready before you start pairing.

Look at the motions of your stock. The excreta

from healthy birds is black, with tips of white, which denote the passage of uric acid, and which is the natural way of elimination of this acid from the birds. Signs of poor condition are feathers carried loosely, birds inactive, sitting at the end of the perches with feathers puffed out like a ball. Lack of song in the male birds, and no calling from the hens. Looseness in the excreta, and the same being of a different colour. Birds with an unusually large appetite for soft food, and eating very little seed. The causes of loss of condition are of course numerous, but the principal ones are lack of fresh air, fluctuating temperatures, draughts, insufficient exercise.

MAKING A MATCH

There are some who talk of introducing the birds gradually by setting the cock in a cage near to his wife that is to be, or in one side of a double compartment cage ; others never bother, but when the birds are ready put the cock straightway into the cage of the hen. This is important. Hens breed far better in cages to which they have become accustomed than in strange cages. Three or four days after the birds have been introduced to each other, the nest pan and nesting material may be fixed. The pan at the back, and the nesting material to the wires in front. There are quite a number of different materials which can be used for nesting. With the porcelain or clay nest-pan, a felt lining is always used, clean dry moss, manilla rope cut into short lengths, and well teazled out. Medicated horse or cow hair, deer hair, clean dry grass, are all suitable materials. Cotton waste should not be used, as it packs down tight, and prevents

B*

ventilation in the nest ; another disadvantage of cotton waste or wool is that being so absorbent, the nest will not be very presentable after the young birds reach the age of 12 or 14 days. Ventilation through the nest is necessary. Three or four more days pass, the nest is made, and one morning an egg is seen in the nest. It should be removed, as should the second and third eggs, and all three may be returned either on the night of the third day or the morning of the fourth.

The former is the best plan, as the eggs are more likely to chip altogether than if not returned till the fourth morning. The first three eggs are cold when returned to the nest, the fourth is never cold, therefore if the first three are returned on the evening of the third day they are warmed up and start level with the fourth, and so the chicks all hatch about the same time on the thirteenth night or fourteenth morning from the return of the eggs. In the early part of the season incubation is generally a few hours longer than when the days are warm and long.

PREPAREDNESS THE BEST DEFENCE

To be best able to fight the red mite one should look ahead. Therefore when the eggs are returned to the nest, they and the nest should be well dusted with insect powder. Red mite are no longer the menace they once were, and may be completely eliminated by the application of the anti-mite sprays and washes now available.

If the cock is being run with more than one hen, he should be removed at night when the eggs are returned to the nest. He can then be introduced to his second wife, and the same procedure followed as we have detailed for the first hen.

There are some fanciers who never leave a cock with a hen after she has gone to nest. They are wise when he is run with more than one, but when one cock to one hen is the rule, we like to leave them together all the time, unless it should happen the cock interferes with the hen during incubation, or will not do his bit in feeding the youngsters when they come.

MODERN FEEDING METHODS

That last sentence leads us to the thought that the youngsters will need feeding, but before we talk about their food we will say something about that of the old birds.

For a month before they are mated the old birds should be given some egg food, or one of the proprietary prepared substitutes for it every other day, in addition to the daily seed which should consist of summer rape given as the staple food in the seed hopper and a mixture of canary, inga, and maw seed in the seed drawer or tin. Green food should be given every day.

In these latter days cod liver oil food has been largely used by fanciers. Cod liver oil food is like whisky—it needs to be used with discretion. It should never be fed regularly every day, except to bring very backward birds into condition for the breeding season, or to sickly birds. In such cases it may be used every day, also for a day or two before and after birds come back from a contest. It may be given to the birds twice a week when they are newly paired, and three times a week during the breeding season, or every day if given mixed in equal proportions with the ordinary canary food. During the moulting season it may also be used as during the breeding season. Cod liver oil food is very heating and forcing. That is why it must be used with discretion.

FEEDING THE BABES

When the young birds make their appearance the ordinary seed diet may be continued, but in addition soaked seed should be fed three times daily. Hens are very fond of soaked seed and will often feed on it when they refuse to do so on the ordinary egg food, or other soft food.

Its method of preparation is as follows :—Equal parts of canary, rape, and hemp seed should be put into a big jam jar, covered with cold water, and soaked for twenty-four hours. When it has been soaking twelve hours it should be well stirred up with a spoon, the water drained off, and some fresh water poured over it. When it has soaked a whole day it should again be stirred, the water drained off, fresh water put to it, again stirred, and drained. Then it is ready to be given to the birds. So as to keep a regular supply one lot should be set soaking in the morning, and another at night each day. Thus that which is set soaking in the morning will be used the next morning, and the evening lot will be used the next evening.

GREEN FOOD

We believe strongly in green food, and fresh green food should be given to the breeding stock every day, and when there are young birds, three times a day— watercress, lettuce, groundsel, chickweed, and dandelion are all good, but do not use too much of the latter, especially after the early spring time. Green food should always be well washed in slightly salted water before being given to the birds. Care must be taken never to give frosted green food, and at each time of feeding all stale green food should be removed from the cages. Many cases of inflammation of the bowels are due to stale green food, and stale egg food. Moral: Let all food be fresh.

FIXING THE RINGS

Rings should be fitted when droppings appear on the rim of the nest, usually about 5 or 6 days after hatching. At this stage the hen has ceased to clean out the nest so diligently and is less likely to remove the rings. The "British Roller Canary Association" and also its affiliated Roller Canary Clubs insist upon all birds bred by their members being rung. We give illustrations of how the ringing is performed. The three front claws are put together, and the ring slipped over them, then up over the back claw, which is pressed close to the leg.

Evening is the best time for ringing the birds, as the hens are most restful, and do not try to remove them. It is wise to smear the rings with some excreta when they are on the legs of the birds. This dims them, and the hens do not notice them. It is the brightness of the rings which attracts the hens, and causes them to pull them off. Watch must be kept for a day or two to see that the rings have not been pulled off.

When the young are three weeks of age, the thoughts of the old birds will turn towards another family, and a clean nest pan should be hung on the opposite side of the breeding cage to the previous one, and some nesting material provided. Here it may be said that the nest with the young should be renewed once each week whilst the babes are occupying it.

The hen will go to the nest sometimes before her first lot of babes are able to take care of themselves, but the cock bird, if given the opportunity, will generally take

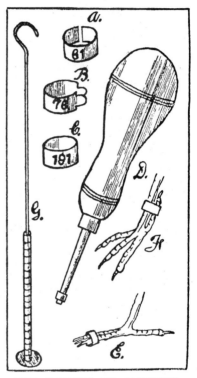

THE RINGING OF CANARIES.

A B C, Types of Rings. D, Tool for Rubbering when rubber is pulled over Ring. E F, Mode of Ringing. G, Ring Holder.

charge of the babes, and tend them well, until they can fend for themselves, which they should do when a month old, and can then be removed to the flight cages.

CHAPTER IV

EDUCATION BEGINS

THE flight cages to which the young birds are removed should not be in the breeding room, but in another room, and in that room should be a good schoolmaster, so as to teach the young how to sing.

The food given to the birds may be the same as that given in the breeding cage, and should be continued right through the moulting period.

It is most essential to success in competition work that the birds should be put under the schoolmaster at the earliest age possible. When from six to eight weeks old, the cocks may be detected by the swelling of their throats when attempting to sing. They should be removed from the hens, and placed in another flight. Some cage them off in small cages, but this is not wise before the completion of the moult as the exercise which the birds obtain in the flights gives them strength and muscle.

Further instructions as to the management and training of the young birds will be found in the chapter dealing with " Training Rollers for Competition."

WINTER MANAGEMENT

When the breeding season is over, the cages should all be thoroughly cleansed by being washed out, disinfected, and dried. The room also should be cleaned, the ceiling and walls whitewashed, and the floor well scrubbed. The hens may then all be kept in this room away from the cocks, and any cocks that prove useless for competition work may be kept there until they are sold, either as songsters or for breeding stock.

During the winter months the hens, and the cocks, may be given canary and rape seed as their staple food in the hopper, and the mixed seeds in the seed drawer may be given every other day. Soft food, such as egg food, cod liver oil food, or one or other of the prepared proprietary foods, may be given twice a week.

Green food should be given whenever obtainable, a slice or two of sweet apple, or of boiled carrot, may be given when green food cannot be found, or even by way of a change.

Let the birds have free access to a grit pan, unless you use sand on the cage bottoms. Keep cuttle fish bone always hanging in the flights. Supply fresh water daily, and keep all drinking and feeding utensils absolutely clean. Give a little tonic in the drinking water once or twice a week during the moult, and also through the winter. Supply them with a bath once or twice a week.

Let the birdroom be well ventilated, but avoid all draughts. Thus catered for, your breeding stock should keep well, and be very fit when the breeding season approaches.

KEEPING THE RECORDS

It is essential for the proper management of a stud that

the recording of the pedigrees of the birds in a Stud Register or Stock Book should be carefully kept.

The daily happenings in the stud may be noted in a small memorandum book or a card chart, and then transferred to the Stock Book once a week, or at such intervals as are convenient.

Beyond its value as a record of the pedigree of every bird in the stud at any given moment, past or present, it is deeply interesting, and very helpful, in many ways. It will show all the pairings, with ring numbers of old and young, dates of mating, laying, and hatching, together with the results of each nest, of each pair, and the whole stud for the season. If properly kept, it will contain records of all sensational birds, all birds that have been afflicted with illness, and also those that have died either from accidents or disease.

All records in connection with the pedigree of each bird should be entered fully into the Stock Book, so that a quick reference can be made if required. A small book should be prepared, or a breeding chart should be made. The most convenient form is a large thick piece of white cardboard; this can be ruled to provide a column for each cage, allowing space for three nests from each pair of birds. The ring numbers of both male and female should be placed in the first square, and as the work of the season progresses, notes can be made in the respective columns regarding results from each pair, such as time set, time due to hatch, number of young birds hatched, and number raised, together with the ring numbers of the young birds themselves, in each succeeding nest. Later, all these particulars can be entered in the Stud Register, which becomes a permanent record of each year's work.

CHAPTER V

ON BUILDING A STRAIN

THERE is not space in a small book of this character to go into all the details of establishing a strain. We can only refer our readers to articles on in-breeding which appear in " Cage Birds." These are published from time to time and they go fully into the subject. There are those who say in-breeding is wrong. It is if improperly followed, but not if conducted on rational lines. We are so convinced that in-breeding is the royal road to success that we say anything may be achieved in the way of stock-breeding by following out the principles as laid down by our contributors.

How is it possible to have a strain unless one does in-breed? The mating of birds gathered from here, there and everywhere will not create a strain. All the great breeders of Roller Canaries in Germany held their own strains, strains which were famous for different qualities of song.

Woerz, a great breeder, says:—" Inbreeding is the shortest way for the safe inheritance of certain, nay, of all peculiarities, and for the improvement of the strain. No breeder can do without it. By its means can faults or imperfections connected with the strain be quickly remedied. But one must keep the in-breeding within bounds, and the greatest care has to be taken in the choice of breeding material."

Breeders such as Rosenbach, Volkmann, Engelhe, Truto, Seifert, Bergmann, Erntyes, Wooje, Jacquemin, and others who have made great strains, all practised and preached in-breeding.

WHAT IT WILL DO

In-breeding, properly followed, will improve the song of the Roller Canary, and by the same process of selection and mating may the outward form of the birds be improved. Indeed, it is possible by such to create a strain of Rollers which for song and dominant form will repeat season after season with surprising and pleasing regularity, until the breeder can claim, within the space of several seasons, a super strain of Rollers. Let us consider these factors. Take vigour, this is most important, and in every description of breeding vigour is the first selection. Breed vigour into your stock in an intensive form and sickness will seldom worry you. It is my opinion that wild birds are so intensively bred that vigour has prevailed for centuries and the weaklings have long since passed away. Select your breeding stock from sound healthy birds. Never breed with weak or sickly birds, and you can in-breed for ever.

It is in-breeding in families or flocks which has caused our native songsters to breed so absolutely true to vigour, size, shape, colour and marking that the young repeated their inherited factors with regularity. Think of the regularity of marking seen in the Goldfinch, the Chaffinch, Bullfinch, Siskin and other British birds. It is all the result of in-breeding. " Birds of a feather flock together " is an old saying, but there is much in the remark which accounts for wild birds seldom crossing.

Different breeds of wild birds were developed ages ago when birds were in very limited quantities. If such purity of colour and marking was accomplished by wild birds consanguineously mating, just imagine what can be accomplished by man with scientific selection and mating. We have not to grope in the dark, for the most difficult problems of breeding have long since been proved by our forefathers, though unfortunately few have followed the wise and clever breeders of old.

The more intensively one breeds the more does one stamp upon the strain the qualities it possesses, and the greater these qualities the greater the success of the strain. If we take song it is easy to produce by careful selective in-breeding a race, or strain, that will be all-conquering in the contests.

How is one to follow the advice given by all the great masters of the past: "Keep to one strain", unless they in-breed? Immediately strange blood is introduced into a stud away goes all the distinctive characters of the strain. He who would succeed with the Roller Canary must in-breed. By strict selective breeding, and keeping a careful record of all stock bred and the performances of the best birds, it is possible to achieve success of the highest degree.

Breeders have now succeeded in improving the appearance of the Roller. When "The Roller Canary" was first written the majority of Rollers were nondescript green or heavily variegated birds. There is now a large proportion of clear or lightly marked birds bred each year and there is a growing section of the fancy which is cultivating the newer colours such as opal or red factors in their stock. Although there is still a great deal of work to be done in these varieties, some first class white ground birds have been bred which are quite capable of holding their own at the singing contests.

CHAPTER VI

AUTUMN MANAGEMENT AND TRAINING

In this chapter the well-known judge, M. Jacquemin, details the necessary procedure from the end of the breeding season up to the time when the birds should be able to hold their own in the Singing Competitions.

WHEN the breeding season is at its final stage, we must see to the most important part of our hobby—the training of the young cocks. do not believe in putting young cocks too early in single cages ; as long as they sing quietly I leave them in the flight cages, 15 cocks in a flight 7 feet long and 2 feet deep and 2 feet high, and feed them on canary and rape seed, with every day some crushed hemp seed, mixed seed and green food.

About the middle of August I put some of them in single cages, and give them as their regular food canary and rape mixed, egg food once a week, and one day mixed seed consisting of hemp, linseed, groats, millet, inga and maw seed, also now and then a little chickweed or lettuce.

The cages I leave open, so that the birds can see each other for at least a week, as I find that they settle down better than if they are darkened down at once. It is a great mistake to shut them up at once, you must let them find the way to their seed and water ; the mixed seed may be placed on the sand tray.

Place the tutor in the room amongst the young cocks, and you will be surprised how quickly they settle down to their new life in the small cages.

After a week or two, according to their progress, put a partition between the cages, but should they be too restless take the partition away again for a few days. If not, leave them and watch and listen to their song, or rather twittering.

WATCH AND TAKE NOTES

Now is the time to watch your young stock. Take all the ring numbers and have them on the cages, also make a list with the ring numbers on, and have it always handy when you listen to your birds. Those which sing (twitter) with closed beak mark " good " or " deep " on your list, others which sing with open beak mark " noisy " or " high." You can hear them when they are ever so young. In a deep bird you can see the throat move and only a roll comes out of it, but if you hear a lot of " S—sis," you can put him down as high.

Put the deep ones together and also the high ones, but do not take them away altogether, as you must listen for another week or two before you send them away to another tutor. Keep on marking your list from one week to another ; you can partly tell after a few days which bird will be your champion, also put down on your list which bird always sings first.

After a few weeks you begin to distinguish the different Rolls or Glucks, and you must mark the tones on another list. Just mark it H.R., B.R., W.Gl., or H.B., and so on, and you will find the birds you marked early on your list as deep or high, as the case may be, will be your best deep or high birds; also it is good practice towards judging your own or other fanciers' birds.

As your birds begin to shape into the different tours you will have to examine them and your list closely together. If you have several tutors, so much the better for you. Place those young cocks which follow the particular old bird's song with him, the remainder with another, and put them in the places you have to train them in.

GLASS DOORS AND LIGHT CURTAINS

Now put birds into cages with glass doors and light curtains. If you have only one good old cock, put your deeper-singing birds quite close to him and the higher ones you have to darken down or let them take their chance by themselves. The higher ones I put on the bottom or side row and place a piece of paper in front for extra darkening. I do not myself take the higher ones away together, but keep them so that they can hear the tutor bird, and darken them down. In this way you have a higher percentage of good birds than if you discard them.

KEEP TO ONE STRAIN

If you have birds with too many faults, you must take them away or you may spoil the good ones. It does not happen so easily if you breed only one class of birds; you have then a better percentage of good birds because they harmonise better together; you can hear more of the strain in them.

A fancier who breeds with a mixture of birds

c

from several different strains will have a poor percentage
of good birds.   Further, it takes longer to separate
the good from the bad, and in the end he will only have
high ones left after all his trouble.

If a breeder is possessed of plenty of room, I advise
him to separate his young cocks into different rooms,
according to their quality.   For this purpose you must
have several tutors at your disposal, and you must place
the young cocks with the old bird which they follow
the nearest in song.

A USEFUL EXPERIMENT

This experiment you can also practice with a few
young cocks if you want to introduce a tour or a new
style of song.   This applies only to a man with plenty
of young cocks, but it is worth trying, and, if you are
lucky to get only one good young cock, it pays you for
your extra trouble.

As your birds progress in song, you must begin hand-
ling them, which means you have to take several of
them into another room and put an old one among
them.   He will start the concert, and by this you will
get them to sing anywhere and in strange surroundings,
which will be to your good when they are judged
later on.

It is wise to take a couple of young cocks into another
room, quite away from the others.   When they sing, you
will think you have another bird to listen to; it makes
such a lot of difference to sit in a quiet room and have
the birds before you.   The sound has a quite different
effect; also you can hear them better, and it is another
big step towards making them free songsters.

TRAINING FOR THE SHOWS

A few weeks before the show, put your birds in contest cages. First leave the door open, and, after a day or two, shut it. Treat them just the same as explained before, the only difference is now to handle them more in playing about in other rooms or, better still, take one or two to a friend's house and entice them to sing in the shortest possible time, because the quick singing bird will, nine times out of ten, be the winner in a contest.

Still make notes on your list as to which bird sings his song throughout or in sections, or which one always sings first. With this one, let him sing his song and no more, as you are likely to spoil him in having too much song out of him, for then he will get excited, and will bring all his faults. As long as a bird sings his tours nicely, let him do so, and no more ; he will get his reward before the judge ; never mind what he sings after judging. This applies only to birds you intend to show.

Birds trained like this will get into the money time after time. A few birds just ready for the show bench, singing their song in a nice quiet way, and only slightly faulty, will be the winners ; they are just ready at the right time, and win, even if they do not do much at later shows.

c*

CHAPTER VII

THE DEVELOPMENT OF SONG

THE development of the different song tours begins as soon as the young cocks are in the flight cages. They start when they are six weeks old, and, in some cases, even earlier. In the elementary stage only a gentle twittering is noticeable, but, day by day, it becomes louder and stronger.

The young bird's first moult does not hinder him in this. He practises daily with diligence, and makes progress, and, even in these early days, while the birds are still in the moult, one can already distinguish plainly in some of the more forward birds certain tours in their song.

THE INFLUENCE OF THE MOULT

If, as occasionally happens, a breeder possesses a young cock who, in spite of being a sound, healthy bird, misses his first moult, he will discover that this bird, after a very short course of study, will outstrip all his companions, and bring out his tours like an adult. The conclusion is, therefore, obvious that the moult hinders development of the song. It is a question of duration, that is, whether the bird renews his feathers slowly or quickly, and it will be found that those which have made the most progress in the moult will show the greatest advance in their song.

36

Age has nothing to do with it, for birds of the same age who vary in their moult will vary accordingly in their song development, a fact which can be verified during any breeding season, for it will be found that older learners having a long moult are outstripped by quick moulting younger ones. With an even moult all round, the older birds naturally are the best developed in body as well as song.

As it is mostly the custom to keep the birds in the freedom of the flight cages during the moult, and to cage them off only after completion, it follows that the song develops while they are already in the flights. So long as loud and distinct notes or passages are not distinguished above the twitterings of the beginner, the birds may be left quietly alone.

THOSE FAULTY NOTES

The first of the notes which strike the ear as disagreeable are the faults in the song which, later on, when the bird is fully developed, make it necessary to isolate him from the general company. Quite early we may hear sharp flutes, for these are the first to break in upon the soft warbling. After this we get a lengthy bell, which gradually becomes longer in delivery and harder, if not finally quite sharp.

A short soft bell from which the bird descends to another tour is no fault, and does not jar, but if a young bird brings his bell frequently and at length, the tour almost always develops into a fault, sometimes even a downright bad one, and such a songster may spoil the whole school. By his unceasing ringing he urges on his companions, and, as he brings it out by the yard, as it were, nothing but loud bell is heard after a short time. This long, loud bell tour may well be reckoned as the worst of all faults, for such a bird thinks he can never do enough of it, and, in many cases, he will keep it up for pretty well a minute.

Following on the above-mentioned two bad faults, sharp flutes and sharp bell, we very quickly hear the rasping sound of the Aufzug. This is a fault for which most breeders do not isolate if it is not too lengthy, the reason being that with deep-voiced songsters this tour of breath-recovery will gradually dwindle away. It, nevertheless, has always a jarring effect upon the ear.

THE DISAGREEABLE NASAL NOTES

Then, again, we have the nasal notes. If this fault be confined to a few of the birds, they are taken away from the school, but if nearly all have the fault, the breeder cannot isolate them, and must leave the whole lot together, for it is often the case that when the nasal is first detected he will scarcely be able to find one clear-voiced bird. For this reason the opinion rules among breeders that the nasal is as catching as the plague.

All nasal, *i.e.,* harsh and impure, generally hoarse, tours, are very disagreeable, but deep flutes are the worst when spoilt by this hoarseness; such birds must be taken away, for this kind of loud flute is so penetrating in tone that it stands out conspicuously, ugly and persistent, while the others are singing, and absolutely spoils the effect of the whole orchestra.

The last faults, and most difficult to handle, are known as Schnetter and Zitzit. Loud sharp Schnetter sounds like a loud, hard rattle or castanets, and bell

Schnetter is a sharp bell, degenerating further into a rattle. Then there is soft Schnetter, which the novice mistakes for soft Aufzug, but which the expert knows is Schnetter pure and simple.

Zitzit is a bad habit which, perchance, the bird may lose ; nevertheless, he must be banished from the school. If he is inclined to let it drop he will have to do so in the company of the other banished ones.

SEPARATE THE BAD FROM THE GOOD

Birds that have the faults above referred to must be separated from the good songsters as early as possible, and placed in another room out of earshot; the chances that such birds may become decent songsters are very meagre, further, it is waste of time and effort to place them under a tutor. Let them sing their good and bad tours together to their hearts' content, and take the first opportunity to dispose of them.

One is often advised to darken these birds deeply, so as to suppress or stifle the fault, but this will not answer any good purpose, for the breeder who adopts the plan is thereby induced to keep the faulty birds in the same room as the others, thinking that by this means the faults will be less audible. One must bear in mind, however, that the birds cannot be kept in the dark during the whole day; they must, at least for one hour every day have light and freedom, even if it only be at feeding times, for then they should have quite an hour of broad daylight accorded to them, so that they may satisfy their needs in a proper manner.

DISCORD AMIDST HARMONY

When they are regularly fed, they get to know the time when the welcome light will be vouchsafed to them, as they fidget about from perch to perch, chirping and twittering the while. When they have filled their needs the little ne'er-do-wells begin with joy to warble forth their thanksgiving; the signal is given, the band starts and away they go in full strength, sharp flutes, sharp bell, Aufzug, Schnetter, and all the rest, and the performance is so loud and penetrating that the breeder hears it at the other end of his dwelling, and hurries off to darken them down again, so that his good birds may no longer hear this questionable music.

HOW TO OBTAIN GREAT PLEASURE

The best way is to place these throw-outs in a distant room, and let them enjoy life. The breeder, then, has his pleasure in his better songsters far less hindered than when his room contained the blunderers, whose faults even darkening down would not completely silence. Having dealt with the development of bad faults, we turn our thoughts to those tours which bring joy to the trainer.

THE FIRST AND FINEST TOUR

We will suppose that all the birds in the room are bred from first prize parents, and the breeder prides himself in the belief that the offspring will be as good as their ancestors in quality.

The birds are healthy, and they make fast progress

in their studies. One day he hears the hollow roll, queen of tours, the tour that gives the song its intrinsic value, and without which there can be no talk of good song. The tour we hear first, therefore, is this, the finest.

At first it is short, then quick, and gradually lengthening out, of medium pitch, rising and falling soft and clear ; very soon afterwards we hear the first beats of the deep Hollow Roll (rrrou). When the "hollow," as we call it, comes out well in this stage, the breeder knows he has won his object ; "hollow" songsters are ever sought after. Only one care now remains, namely, as to whether he is going to discover a good strong Knorre (Bass), but he must wait patiently, for although Bass is not the latest arrival, yet it does not make its appearance in the young birds until September.

HOLLOW BELL AND HOLLOW ROLL

After Hollow Roll we very quickly get Hollow Bell, which also rises and falls on the same pitch with the same vowel sounds, but, of course, without the roll of the "rrr." Deep Hollow Bell "ou, ou, ou," is commonly, but incorrectly, marked Schockel, which tour we shall describe later.

Very soon we shall hear Bell Roll with a clear roll on "rrree," and a nice short soft bell "lllee," also tender flute notes, "tee, tee, tee," and the deeper "dou, dou, dou." These flutes are an ornament to the song, and heighten the value of the bird. To the well-attuned ear of the musical breeder there is no greater delight than listening to a number of good birds with a pure song heightened by deep tender flute notes which shine out in soft relief, now here, now there, like costly jewels, while the bent Hollow Roll long drawn out, is rising and falling.

In the course of time the curving and heaving of the song becomes longer and more powerful, the Hollow Roll, Hollow Bell, Bell Roll, Bell, and Flutes all getting daily more perfect.   However, in spite of all this it strikes one sometimes as though the song were not making progress, because there are still wanting certain valuable tours which the breeder for song wishes to have in his birds.

CHAPTER VIII

GLUCK AND WATER ROLL

THERE are certain prize winning tours which are
only bred by speciality breeders who have an
exceptional love for them. These are Gluck and
the Water Roll tours, and they may both seriously
degenerate in the course of the year.

To many minds Gluck as an embellishment is a
superfluity, for even if it be perfect, clear in tone, slow
and quiet, " gluck, gluck, gluck " (better written
" glook "), it is no greater ornament than deep flutes ;
it heaves up in the song in a similar manner, but in it
there is lacking the melancholy, plaintive appeal of
flutes on " dou."

TOURS THAT DEGENERATE

Flutes compensate fully for Gluck, they are easier
to cultivate, and do not degenerate, or very rarely,
whereas Gluck, even with the slightest alteration in the
feeding during the rearing period, will drop into the
worst faults.

From parents singing good Gluck there arise in the
youngsters such things as kleck, kleck, klack, klack, and
the fearsome chop and chap. If the young birds develop
these dreadful tours the whole of the strain goes over-
board, for what breeder cares to continue with such
birds, even if a few of them should not have degenerated

to quite such an extent? He must get rid of all his cocks, the choppers for what they will fetch; the hens also he cannot keep, and thus all his trouble and expense for one whole year have been wasted, and he must put his hand deep down in his pocket to start again with birds of a good strain. No tour degenerates so much as Gluck.

Water Roll also is as likely to go worse as to become better, and is as little to be recommended as a tour to breed for. If the breeding cocks are very good stock birds, and they are paired up with fair, or even very good, hens, we shall nevertheless hear the youngsters giving voice to things that will certainly not be pleasant hearing.

BEAUTIFUL BUT DANGEROUS

For instance, say the old birds had a lulling (kullering) hollow, a tour which decided the purchase on account of the charm of its delivery. Their tours were a good bass, flutes, deep hollow, and also a deep lulling, clear on " ou," no weak watery effect. This deep kuller, which is really beautiful and quite arrests attention, carries its danger with it, for even with suitable hens the youngsters bring out all sorts of weak watery stuff, for which no name can be given.

Breeders, in whose hands such birds do not degenerate, gain much both from a material and an ideal standpoint ; it certainly rewards an expert to listen to birds which sing the hollow in pure kullering or kollering form, but the goal is only reached by first-class, experienced breeders and trainers, for the reason that the kollering and kullering tours have all got the water beat, one may say they are a blending of Hollow Roll and Water Roll. This combination, in the hands of inexperienced breeders, may resolve itself, again, into Hollow Roll and Water Roll separately. Further, the Water Roll may lose its good qualities and retrograde into weak water and broad wish-washy stuff, and as the song of the youngster develops this watery stuff becomes more and more apparent, and he must be taken away from the school.

Rippling tours on " o " and " ou " are good. Birds of this category should be placed close to one another, and they should have a fair songster as tutor with a fully-developed kullering tour, so that they may have good instruction and support, and, in their turn, become first-rate songsters.

WHEN BASS DEVELOPS

Bass develops at about the end of September or the beginning of October ; at first there is a short " rrr," which soon becomes louder and stronger, and then the breeder will have an idea as to what the quality will be. The bass tones knorr and knourrr are good, and birds possessing them may be used for further breeding purposes or for sale.

We get also a soft deep bass, but not on " o " or " ou," as above, but more of an " a," as in " arr," a variety which is still good, and, although a sensitive breeder may perhaps talk disparagingly of this so-called knarre, many would be pleased if they had such bass in their song.

The last of the good tours which the birds lay hold of is Schockel, and to develop it a schoolmaster possessing it is absolutely necessary. This tour may be dormant in the bird for a twelvemonth without making its appearance, and, finally, under the leadership of a tutor, he will suddenly bring it out.

True Schockel is in the same musical pitch as deep flutes, and only birds who have deep flutes bring it out, in its manner of delivery it is practically deep flutes in faster time. In order to cultivate Schockel you have to select birds who repeat their deep flutes at least six to eight times consecutively, and if you give them a tutor with true Schockel, not Hollow Bell, and leave them for a long period under his tuition, they will build up the Schockel out of their deep flutes through the fashion of the delivery, but without a tutor you can never attain to this.

EXPERT VIEWS ON THE GLUCK TOUR

With regard to the assertion that deep flutes should take the place of Gluck, and that Gluck is superfluous, many will agree with the following remarks by another expert. He writes as follows:—" There is no doubt that deep flutes are a fine acquisition, and enchant the ear; every breeder should strive to bring good deep flutes into his song. However, a well-delivered Gluck or Gluck-roll is not less beautiful, and no one having these tours in his strain would ever wish them to disappear.

" The ideal Gluck is reached when it is full, mellow, and deep, rising and falling, a veritable delight to the ear. The beauty of the song cannot be denied. Moreover, the fine Gluck tours which characterize these strains are accompanied by beautiful deep, plaintive flutes, good bass, etc., a proof that deep flutes can be cultivated along-side the Gluck tours.

"The fears of easy degeneration of the Gluck tours I do not share ; it may happen, but not any more often than with other tours, and, in my opinion, the appear-ance of Chop can, at any rate, only take place after several years, and if the breeder omits to be careful in his selection of birds for breeding purposes.

"With the best strains, I have not discovered a single case of degeneration, although I have kept in close touch with them for seven years. Neither have I found that a change of diet, for instance, a course of stimulating food, has had any lasting influence on the delivery of the Gluck tours. To be sure, the tours were not so soft at breeding time, but this is so with all the tours, especially as regards bass. When breeding time is over, or after the moult, the tours, with very few exceptions, will resume their former softness and fullness.

WHEN DETERIORATION SETS IN

"When deterioration in a Gluck strain sets in it is almost always on account of too close in-breeding (father to daughter, etc.); this re-acts more in Gluck than in any other tour. It is certainly advisable not to over-look bringing in well-selected fresh blood after a certain time, both in Gluck and Water strains, otherwise ugly variations will creep in.

To be successful in contests in this country it is necessary to breed birds which sing the Gluck tours. Nevertheless, care must be taken, as too much emphasis on breeding for Gluck can lead to a deterioration in the general tone of the song. Breeding for Water tours is especially prejudicial to the quality of the Hollow tours and for this reason Water tours are not highly valued in England, although most English Rollers sing a water roll of sorts.

CHAPTER IX

TRAINING ROLLERS FOR COMPETITIONS

THE training of the Roller Canary is, of course, a most interesting process, and occupies about three months; breeders are not all alike in the time they take to train their birds. One will cage off early from the flights, while another will delay the operation; or it may be that the birds are backward either by nature or by reason of the lack of continual, steady tuition through the available schoolmaster going off song in the moult, and no substitutes being forthcoming for some time.

It goes without saying that the longer a young bird can be kept in the flight the better chances he has of coming safely through his first moult; of expanding his frame, and becoming a robust youngster.

The tutor is kept near the flight in a cage and song-box by himself. If a youngster becomes quarrelsome, or if he develops sharp or harsh notes or frequent high calls, he should be taken away. To minimize these troubles, or to prevent them, it will be found effective if the flight is shaded, either by a curtain or by darkening the room.

Some cage off the cocks almost as soon as the sexes are discovered; others cage them off as soon as they show livelier attempts at song. The birds are put into small wire cages, and the cages are placed in boxes or cabinets provided with doors. These cabinets almost exclude the light, some entirely so, and the birds are ranged so that the tutor is in the centre.

48

The Training Cage shown on page 50, and also the Cabinet, can be made with any kind of wood to the given sizes, but hard wood, like pitch pine, is preferable, and, when varnished, this will have a very neat appearance. When you have your young birds through the moult, place the cocks in the cages, being careful to place the ring numbers on the cabinets, for this will enable you to find any particular bird by referring to your stock book.

A VALUABLE SUGGESTION

After placing the birds in the cabinets, leave the doors open at first to make sure they find their feeders and drinkers, and let the doors remain open for at least two days. On the third day close one door, the following day partly close the next door, and the succeeding day close all up.

Be sure you have plenty of fresh air in the room in which you are going to keep them. Open the cabinets, and give fresh food and water the first thing every morning, and leave the cabinets open for an hour. Open the doors again at noon for half an hour, and then close until evening.

When you hear one or more of your young birds singing in the darkness open the doors immediately and let them sing their song. Listen very critically for any bad faults, and when they are finished close the doors.

The song box I use is a roomy one, with three holes at the back about $\frac{1}{4}$ in. in diameter, and the doors are so constructed that when closed there is a space of about one-eighth of an inch at each side, allowing of the

D

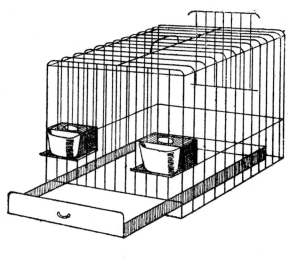

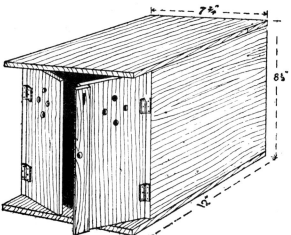

Singing or Training Cage and Cabinet.

passage of air and light. With this and the apertures at the back the bird is never in total darkness.

Another design of cage is the shutter cage, combining cage and box in one, being a box cage with two wooden doors to close in front after the pattern of the official show-cage.

ARRANGING THE SONG BOXES

The birds should be arranged in rows as close together as possible, and if there are many it is better that the tutor should face them, also in his song-box.

As I do not use song boxes except for special purposes, as for a bird in a sitting room when he is generally open, or for a sick one, I describe what I consider to be a simpler system. The birds in their small wire cages are ranged in racks, bookshelf fashion, with two curtains of green casement material suspended in front, one about three inches in front of the other to regulate the depth of shade. If the room has venetian blinds one curtain is sufficient as a rule.

The partition between the cages should be of stout cardboard, thin planed wood, or metal ; wood possibly is the best, as the metal is rather cold. These partitions should come well to the tops and the backs of the cages, and in front they should come out flush with the outside level of the feeding glasses, so that the birds cannot get a view of one another. If the cages rest on rods instead of shelves it may be well to lay sheets of brown paper thereon, to overhang an inch or so in front, and hang down the full depth at back. Have the upper and lower ranges as close as possible, say, half an inch to an inch. In this way you have no boxes to clean out, the birds are closer together, you can shift them about more easily and more quickly; in fact, they are altogether more easily managed.

Place the tutor so that he has two on each side, three above and three below, in all ten birds. Several more can be placed round him, but if you do this it is wise to change the birds about occasionally. If you place your tutor in a song box on a pedestal outside the curtain, regulating his light also properly, you will be able to train a great many more.

HOW TO CAGE OFF

When you cage off a youngster do not shade him at once, nor put in the partition ; let him get accustomed to conditions for a few days, then put up the partition, and, after that gradually shade him. As you cage the birds off you should make a note as to their ages; number the cages according to whether they be first, second or third round birds, and you will not be confused over the feeding.

When you open up your birds in the morning draw out the loose partitions; by this you make them active, and they will not sing, or only a little, if at all. Let them have as much of this as possible, as it keeps them healthy and happy. . Now replace the partitions, and they will start song; close the curtain. Repeat at dinner time.

In the evening, half-an-hour before roosting-time, you may draw the partitions and let them alone until you draw the curtain for the night, leaving the partitions out, or if the days are short you may light up at night, and after they have had half-an-hour's play, replace the partitions, draw the curtain, and gradually lower the light.

You must so regulate the shading that although you keep their song subdued you do not stop them singing altogether. Of course, they will not sing ceaselessly, but you will hear the choir practising more or less during the day.

Now, these are not meant for hard and fast rules, but just merely as guiding principles; the idea is to give the birds as much light and exercise as you can, and to use every means, trick, or stratagem you can think of to keep them from singing in open school, especially during the first few weeks of their training.

A daily rehearsal of ten minutes is good practice, and accustoms them to it; some breeders rehearse three times; methods differ; use your own judgment. You will need to study your birds, you will have them rehearse much longer at times, and this will do them no harm, especially in the cold weather, rather the reverse.

PUPILS WITH FAULTS

Keep a keen ear; remove any high-pitched offender; if a bird seems inclined that way, put him into a dark corner of your rack. If really bad, he must come away altogether, as the faulty tour will vitiate the song of all the others in a day or two; they pick it up in no time, as faulty tours, especially high bell and, in fact, all high notes are easier for them to imitate than the good deep ones.

Sometimes a bird may not be satisfactory for other reasons; as time goes on his style of delivery may not suit, or he many sing a good tour, but repeat it too often, and so cause it to predominate in the others. That bird should be taken away; he may improve by isolation or placing near another, apart from the rest. Sometimes you may have taken a bird away, and may find later on he may go back, but when once he has high bell there is little hope of him being any good in the school.

Keep the best songsters nearest the tutor until they are well advanced. Should your tutor fail you by moulting late, or start early with a long moult, you may find one or two of these youngsters very useful until he comes round again.

When the song has fully developed, study your pedigree, find out the lines of your deepest and purest birds, and mark your hens, so preparing for next season's breeding. Choose your show birds, transfer them to the standard show cages about three weeks before the show, and train them to sing readily to the judge; shift them about the rooms, move them into all sorts of positions, carry them about with you to a friend's house, open them out on the table with a sheet of paper before you as if you were judging.

Reviser's Note

The system of placing training cages on shelves with a curtain in front is now almost universally adopted in preference to song boxes or cabinets as described at the beginning of the chapter, being easier to manage and giving better atmospheric conditions for the birds.

CHAPTER X

SELECTING THE SCHOOLMASTER

FOR a tutor a quiet, slow songster is better than a bold, racy one; a bird weak on his upper tones is better than one who may sing clear but high, and the bird that starts on his lower tours, bass for preference, is better than one who starts on his higher tours.

A bird with faulty high tour or other faults is often good to breed with, coming of good stock and pedigree, but as a tutor he is no good. The tutor should be the best your purse can afford; many fine birds can be bought at their proper value from well-known breeders, but if you limit them to a low figure you cannot expect to get the quality required.

The very finest are priceless; they are very rare, and the owners keep them. They may sometimes be picked up at shows, but many breeders will not risk sending out their very best for exhibition.

High-class birds, however, may be had from fair-dealing British breeders, which, if not of the very highest category, are of close blood relationship to these supreme songsters, and will therefore not only train well, but will breed you first-class birds, and so put you on the right road to excellence.

If your first season does not come up to expectation, remember it is the second season that generally counts; you cannot estimate what you possess until you know the quality of the grandchildren. Perseverance, patience, good judgment, and an attentive musical ear; these are the attributes necessary to a Roller breeder.

One final word as a plea. If you use the song box, take the cage out at least once a day for an hour, and so give the bird an airing and encourage him to hop about and preen his feathers; make his little life a happy one, give him all the liberty and enjoyment you can.

THE FIXING OF THE SONG

It is generally conceded that when the bird has recovered his song after the second moult that song is fixed for good. There can consequently be very little reason why the older birds should not be permitted to enjoy more light and liberty, and live to a good old age.

What are the qualities to seek in a Schoolmaster? Upon this hangs the result of our breeding. After careful, judicious pairing of our birds we may by inattention to this vital question spoil our labour by damaging the song through faulty selection of a tutor.

It is immaterial how a tutor commences his song, so long as it starts with a good tone. Some think that a start on the Bell tours may damage the young cocks by encouraging them to sing only light stuff. This, however, will not occur so readily as in the case of a tutor starting on deep tours, and finishing up with Bell tours, which linger on as if they never wished to finish. Under either such tutor you will always get birds who will start with Bell tours.

It is better to have a tutor who starts with a light Bell or Bell Roll, followed, say, by Hollow Roll or Bass, followed again by Hollow Bell and Flutes, than one which starts with Bass or H.R., and closes with a Bell that never seems to end. The cocks under the first kind of tutor will almost all start with Bell or Hollow Bell, but they will not make their song with Bell a yard long. Such a bird gives also a more pleasing effect than the one which starts deep and finishes up with Bell; the effect of the deep tour is spoilt thereby.

SONGS OF STRENGTH AND BEAUTY

Deep, full-toned tutors who start with their prime tours will bring their whole strength to bear on the lighter, easier ones, and these latter will, therefore, always be high, if not even sharp. On the other hand, those birds who start somewhere on the higher tours will bring their strength and beauty to bear on the succeeding tours, and so bring the song to a good finish.

Beware, however, that your tutor does not start with too long a Bell, nor must he repeat it. Such a tutor must sing correctly, and without a break or interruption, otherwise the youngsters lose the connecting links, and this, when there are many in school, brings desperate confusion.

It is always best when Bell comes in the middle of the song; it makes a pleasing change when followed by Bass or H.R. To understand the effect one needs to listen to a songster who drops into a full round Bass or H.R. after a somewhat high-pitched Bell.

To a trained ear this is a delight, and such a bird, moreover, is a good one to make use of even if his Bell stands out a little too conspicuously in his song.

The next point to consider is as to what faulty tours

may be permitted in a Schoolmaster. Preferably none, of course. Under this heading I do not refer to such things as Zitt or Chop, which are not tours at all but rather jerked out noises, and which happily only a few birds bring out; such faults, of course, no bird should possess, nor any of a similar nature.

There are certain faults which we are ready to excuse in our pets, but they must be sung in the right place, so that they escape being classed among the faulty tours. A bird with an Aufzug at the start is hardly one to be selected; anyhow, it must be very soft, and he must only bring it once, otherwise the whole school will be spoilt, and there will be no end to sorting the birds out.

FAULTS IMPOSSIBLE TO DESCRIBE

Quiet or medium Aufzug, after Bass or just before it, may be permitted without fear, but it must only come out once. The young birds must not be subjected to sharp Aufzug, for after a little while they take up this oft-repeated fault, and the effect is bad, like tearing calico. It is impossible to define Aufzug properly in writing, and it is best to listen to an example.

Birds with very lengthy bell, and which only bring deep tours now and again, should not be used as tutors, neither should those with a lot of sharp, piercing, or nasal flutes, as these birds mar the song to such an extent that it becomes valueless. Weak flutes will not do much damage, and may be permitted; on the other hand, nasal flutes are dangerous.

There are some birds that have not a clear delivery with certain tours, half hoarse, half nasal, one might say indistinct. Opinions differ considerably as to whether they are safe to use. A short, indistinct phrase of this character will do no damage; on the other hand, lengthy Bell and Hollow Bell of this description are very harmful. If one is compelled to use these half-hoarse tours they must be short ones; they will always be imitated and worse. Really hoarse birds should be doctored up in the kitchen, or where they can get warmth and moisture, which are the best means for curing them.

Birds in full breeding condition should not be used as tutors, and the old birds should be taken away during their moult, as they may teach the youngsters many a bad lesson which they otherwise would not have got into their song.

CHAPTER XI

THE INHERITANCE OF SONG

NO doubt exists of the necessity for a tutor in order to educate young birds, although ideas crop up here and there to the effect that education may be brought about without the schoolmaster. These ideas arise from the fact that, in the first place, the bird possesses certain inherited tendencies, and, secondly, he will sing his inherited song without ever having had a cock to guide him; for instance, if in his earliest youth he passes out of the breeder's hands into those of a person who keeps him in absolute solitariness, leaves him entirely to himself, and so permits him to develop his song.

One can take up an attitude on both standpoints, and correctly so; namely, " breeders need no schoolmaster for song development," and, contrariwise, " breeders are bound to have schoolmasters if they wish to develop their song."

It is asserted in some quarters that birds from their earliest youth, even as nestlings, acquire already from the tutor the form of their song, but upholders of this theory seem to lose sight altogether of inborn tendencies. If this were so, it would be needless to concern ourselves about pedigree and inherited qualities, and all we need trouble about would be to look out for a good tutor.

We know that we can only produce birds of high quality from high-class breeding stock, yet no one can correctly assert that the nestlings, even, take up the song of the tutor. It is well known that the father is the best tutor, a fact in favour of my point, for the birds in time will bring out their song, an inherited one.

There is another example of song inheritance—namely, in the case of a hen of a strain representing a variation from the breeder's style of song being crossed with his breeding cocks. The hen transmits, in part or in entirety, the new style of song, but she cannot teach the cocks to sing, so the breeder puts them under a good tutor, maybe their own father. It will then be found that they have not only learnt what their tutor has taught them, but also the pedigree tours of the mother, although they have never heard them.

If the mother be of very fine strain, and the young cocks develop the fine tours inherent in her, in the absence of any performance thereof on the part of the tutor, it will be evident to the breeder that the birds need no special tutor. These facts have also been further verified in the case of a breeder giving to another breeder eggs from a nest in exchange for a nest of his own, the respective strains being foreign to each other.

Now, if the youngsters hatched in the strange room come from a good Bass or Schockel strain, tours not in the repertoire of the birds in this new home, they will nevertheless, when autumn comes, bring out their Bass and Schockel, even though they have had no tutor to help them. It is thus shown that on the face of things no tutor is necessary, yet from what follows it will be seen that, in order to obtain a large percentage of good results among the birds, it is necessary they should be coached by capable tutors.

WHAT CONSTITUTES BEAUTY OF SONG

The fundamental tours of a Canary's song are not the only elements of a good performance, but what constitutes beauty is the order of sequence of the tours, the manner in which they pass one over the other, the bridging over, as it were, the modulation, and the general connectivity, for it is all this that goes to make up a fine song and enhance its value.

Mark well, absence of faults, or faulty delivery, does not indicate value, but what does is method and *style of delivery*.

These special attributes are learnt from the tutor if the young birds are fortunate enough to be brought into contact with one such. It is through the scarcity of tutors on the one hand, and the excessive number of scholars on the other, that so few birds turn out first-class songsters.

When a large number of young birds are on the racks, and the tutor is leading, it is not possible to give them a proper hearing, so much does their warbling drown the song of the old birds. It cannot therefore be expected that one single youngster is capable of taking up the song of his tutor when these tours of a quality so necessary for him to study are overborne by the efforts of the large number around him. The result is that, though the tutor plods on, his efforts are lost, as not one single cock hears him properly.

If, in order to surmount this difficulty, several tutors

are placed among the birds, their song will, of course, dominate. As the tutors do not sing the same tour at the same time, but change about, one singing this tour and another that, the result is that the youngster is at the same disadvantage, as the individual tours are lost to him by reason of the strong volume of sound with, to him, the confused interchanges.

INDIFFERENT RESULTS EXPLAINED

This explains the generally indifferent results of large breeders, notwithstanding their care in providing their birds with good tutors. In the smaller breeding rooms there is often a surprisingly large percentage of cocks which develop into first-class songsters in cases where they are placed under a really good tutor.

These youngsters have been fortunate enough to have a first-class bird to listen to, and also to benefit by, for although they are with others on the training rack the school is such a small one that their united efforts do not drown the effect of the song of the leader, and thus at all times of the day he is able to lend them direction and support.

Now, if a breeder has a large number of young cocks to train he should not allow more than ten to fifteen for one tutor, and each batch of this number must be kept entirely separate; that is to say, staged in separate rooms, for if these batches are kept in the same room the crossing of the tours, both in old and young, will damage the song.

This system of separation into isolated rooms brings the small fancier up against difficulties; he may be able to manage in different rooms so long as the warmer

weather lasts, but when winter approaches there is the
question of temperature, and for the sake of the birds,
which compared to his hens, are inactive, confined to
small cages, he may be compelled to bring them all into
one comfortably warmed abode. The result will be
that the advantage he has gained will be lost, for the
birds, although well ahead in tours, are not yet fixed in
song, and will consequently vacillate and change about.

REMARKABLE IMITATIVE FACULTY

The imitative faculty of the Roller is remarkable;
for instance, time after time I have found that, in the
case of a year-old cock, which has been used to breed
with, if when he drops into moult he is placed alongside
a cock not moulting, he will take up the new song, so
much so that you will often not be able to distinguish
one from the other.

In some experiments of my own some moulting
cocks in a flight were set apart in a quiet room, and here,
a small company, undisturbed, they entirely forgot their
own song and acquired that of the bird placed in their
hearing. In these cases it was a question each time of
a beautifully bent rich song which seems to have been
especially attractive to the musical sensibility of the
moulting cocks.

If a breeder wishes to obtain the greatest number of
good birds and lacks a sufficient number of separate
rooms, and perhaps of tutors also, let him take the
youngsters bred from his best cock and put them with
him in a room apart, or, failing the parent cock, then
some other first-class tutor. He may thus reckon on
obtaining a small output of good birds.

The general stock may be trained in the ordinary way with several tutors if numbers require it, separating out eventually those birds which are of exceptional promise. If a special room is necessary for the throw-outs, how much more important is it that the young birds of high promise should have one.

Reviser's Note

The point being made in this chapter is that to bring out the best in the young birds it is necessary to use a good schoolmaster, but the quality of song must be bred into the birds.

A good schoolmaster can improve well bred birds, but cannot make good ones out of bad ones.

CHAPTER XII

THE ROLLER'S SONG IN MUSICAL NOTATION

THE natural song of the Canary has been changed from its original form under the efforts of breeders and trainers who have in process of time developed and built up therefrom an artistic song full of charm and beauty. The natural gifts of the bird have been so successfully worked upon that the song to-day is a veritable triumph of art.

To satisfy artistic requirements it may be laid down as a general axiom that as the song progresses higher and lower it should ring out harmoniously, and that during its course no disagreeable tones or phrases should appear.

THE TOURS NOT UNDERSTOOD

The tours of the Roller Canary seem difficult mostly because they require thorough discussion and classification, and this is seldom done. The main problem is that very common factor—variation. The Roller Canary is no different in its inheritance to man. One man sings deep bass, another light-bass, another deep baritone, another light-baritone, another tenor, and so on. This voice problem is a matter of register and confounding to the novice who does not know whether a " tenor " bird is singing Schockel because his deep-voiced bird is singing his hollow bell in a very similar key.

There are other factors to be taken into consideration,

66

for birds vary in other matters as do their owners. Some Canaries are more intelligent than others, they vary in temperament and are consequently different in disposition. You have the vigorous bird who sings in a different style to his weak-chested neighbour. Strains of different delivery help to swell the problems of misunderstanding. Is it any wonder then that there are so many people who are not well versed in the tours of that wonderful bird the Roller Canary?

It is our desire that the information given in " The Roller Canary " should increase the knowledge regarding the song of our birds, so that every lover of Rollers should understand the subject thoroughly. The cult of the Roller is not old in England, we have taken it from the Germans, therefore, the language used in describing the song naturally follows that which has been associated with the bird for hundreds of years on the Continent.

In the present-day songs we have the high, the medium, and the deep passages, called Tours. In the higher tours the music is inferior to the medium, in the deeper tours it is best, so far as purity of tone is concerned. For this reason the widest range of variations is to be found in the deep tours and the narrowest in the high. Also, for the same reason, the middle or medium and the deeper tours are much more valuable than the high ones.

We may therefore classify the melody into three divisions, as follows :—

Higher pitched Tours..............Fair

Medium or middle Tours.........Good

Deep Tours....................Very good

E*

For breeders who have a knowledge of music the compass of the more valued tours is set forth below.

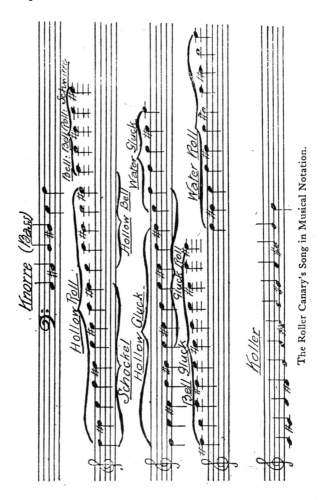

The Roller Canary's Song in Musical Notation.

Flute notes are sung in every pitch shown with the exception of the range given for Bass.

Each single note represents the various degrees of the musical scale on which the tour named can be performed, but it will be well here to remark that birds are not limited to our musical notation, which consists of tones and semitones. Their song has no fixed gradations, but shades into quarter and even eighth-tones, and this, of course, enriches the modulation.

The outside limit for the high tours is given as G sharp above the stave, but if the bird does not sing tenderly and softly, the performance may be faulty, even though it may only reach F sharp.

The complete compass of the song is practically three octaves; the soft rustling tour of former days, known as Schwirre, stretched the compass higher.

ON MEASURING THE BEATS

It is possible to a certain degree to measure the beats in Bell, Hollow Bell, Schockel, Flutes and Gluck, as these tours are syllabic, but with Hollow Roll, Bell Roll, Bass, Koller, Schwirre, and Water Roll, it is scarcely possible, as these tours are more of a tremolo, trilling or warbling nature, so that scarcely any break up into syllables is noticeable.

The style of syllable, the blending of various consonants, and the movement in the different keys constitute certain melodic entities which are called Tours. By analysis of their structure, *i.e.,* their composition, and the manner in which they are built up, as also the ground tone (vowel key sound) on which they are sung, all these tours may be divided into three large groups : —

1. Simple continuous Tours in Rolling form, *i.e.,* tours where the run is not broken by beats; Schwirre, Bell Roll, Hollow Roll.

2. Simple discontinuous Tours in bell-like form; Bell, Hollow Bell, Schockel, Gluck, Flutes.

3. Composite Tours, being partly-rolling, partly bell-like in form; Bass, Koller, Water Roll.

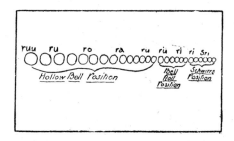

The structure gives us the most essential characteristic of each tour, and the study of this renders it easier for the breeder to recognise and name the tour. The musical value of a tour lies in the quality of its tone, and judges award points accordingly. Tours are good or faulty, according to their tone quality.

Reviser's Note

The chart showing The Roller's song in musical notation is not depicting a tune that the bird sings, but illustrating the range within which each of the tours may be sung. There has evidently been an extension to the range of Hollow Bell since the book was written, as many first class birds today sing their Hollow Bell in the same register as their deep Hollow Roll. Similarly many modern birds sing their Water Gluck deeper than is shown in the chart.

CHAPTER XIII

SIMPLE, CONTINUOUS TOURS IN ROLLING FORM

THE characteristic of all rolling tours lies in the unbroken continuity of the syllables in conjunction with the consonant " r." In all tours with a rolling rhythm, the r is audible, in one more distinctly, in another less so.

A roll without an r is a contradiction; the syllables are formed in the most intimate blending with this consonant, which thus imparts to them the rolling movement. If the r is absent, there can be no unbroken roll, no continuous turning, whirring, sound as the song progresses.

The simplest Roll tours are found on the higher scale, and start with Schwirre as the highest. Then, somewhat lower in pitch, comes Bell Roll, and lower still (medium down to the deepest) comes Hollow Roll.

SCHWIRRE (THE WHIRRING, WHIZZING TOUR)

In the composition of Schwirre the ground tone is " i," blended with " r," and sometimes also " b," and " s," so that it runs in riririri, sririri or sbririri in a continuous fashion.

Its quality depends upon the purity, clearness of the " i," and the force of the consonants " r," " s," and " b." Nevertheless the weakest, thinnest " i " may be good, if performed very softly (pianissimo), and tenderly. The "r" must be lightly breathed, and it must be blended so softly with the "i" interwoven with a subdued "s," that it is scarcely perceptible, just sufficient to maintain the "i" in a state of vibration. The "Sri" sung thus, high and pure, with the vowel full and falling in a long, swinging phrase, forms a charming episode.

This tour ingratiates itself by its soft, placid, melodious character and its silvery tone. Such a Schwirre starts pianissimo, gradually increases to forte, and then passes along down to a wonderful Hollow Roll.

AN ARTISTIC PERFORMANCE

It is difficult to breed such a high placed "i" and at the same time for it to be of such a fine quality. Most of our present-day deep songsters are not able to perform it pianissimo; their Schwirre is rough, sharp, hard, and is therefore a danger. A deep songster, however, who can perform in soft falsetto a pure Schwirre with a fine tone shading is a valuable bird. One must be able to picture in one's own mind such an artistic performance in order to gauge its value.

If Schwirre, although soft and pure, is sung "straight," *i.e.,* on one note, the falling and swelling out as described above being lacking, it is of less value, as also the following:—Vowel "i" not clear, something between "i" and "e" (nasal) Predominance of the "r"; coarse. Predominance of the "s"; sharp. Frequent, distinct accentuation of the "b" sound; hammering.

If other than these three consonants appear in these high notes, such as " dschri," we get Schnetter Schwirre, one of the most dangerous faults in the Roller song.

BELL ROLL

Composition: The ground tone is " i," and the thinner sound " ü." The consonant is " r."

The word " roll " denotes the character of this tour, and " bell " shows the position it occupies on the musical scale. This tour therefore occupies the same position on the register as Bell in contrast with the deeper rolling tour Hollow Roll.

The idea that Bell Roll is so-called because it tinkles and rolls at the same time is incorrect, for a pure Bell Roll is sung in one continuous series " ririri," or " rürürü," whilst Bell is discontinuous (for lack of a better word), and does not roll.

Its quality depends upon the purity of the vowels " i " and " ü," and the force of the " r." The vowel must be nicely rounded so as to manifest tonality; the " r " must not drown the vowel. The tour is of less value if the vowels are indistinct, lacking in purity or too thin, or if they are dominated by the " r " so that the song becomes coarse, dull, nasal, hard or dry. The high vowel " i " sung with open beak and a strong air current, combined with " r " or, " s," results in shrillness. If " sch " is mingled with the " r " and " i " the tour will be shallow and broad.

Bell Roll counts among the higher pitched good tours, and forms the bridge between Schwirre and Hollow Roll.

HOLLOW ROLL

The hollow is founded on ü, o, n, a, ö, e, ä, and the roll is formed by the blending of the consonant r, therefore the syllable is rü, ro, ru, etc. The quality of the tour consists in the purity of the vowel, and the enunciation of the " r." The finest ground tones are ü, o, u and a full round ö; these vowels, possessing of themselves a natural roundness, impart a wonderful fulness and charm to the song.

Vowels a, e, ä are of less value; a is somewhat weak and dull, e and ö (the latter if not full and round) are coarse and heavy, and therefore weaken the tonality; ä is bordering on the nasal, which is risky.

If the " r " is so evident as almost to smother the vowel sound, the tour becomes coarse, hard, and sometimes scratchy; if it is moderate, combined with a deep " u," or " o," the tour runs on, gushing and purling. If the " r " is quite subdued, a soft k, h, and l being heard vibrating, the song becomes noble, charming, lulling (kullering), thus :—Klruhlruhlruhlrohlroh.

This kullering Hollow differs from simple Hollow Roll by reason of these soft, waving, hovering consonants, in deep, full tone, and the almost complete absence of the " r "; it is evidently a development or expansion of Hollow Roll on " u " and " o."

Hollow Roll may, in general, be divided into four series, High, Middle, Deep, and Deepest. The high is of least merit, ground tone " i "; the middle is fair, ground tone " ü "; the deep is good, ground tone " ü " and " ö "; the deepest is the best, ground tone " o " and " u."

When Hollow Roll is sung on one tone only, it is

called "straight," rürürürü, and so on. If it descends
in tone, the syllable changes as it falls, rürürü—rororo,
and so on; this is called falling Hollow Roll. If it

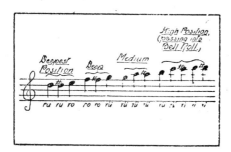

ascends in tone, it is called rising Hollow Roll rororo—
rürürü.

If the bird in one breath sings in varying pitch,

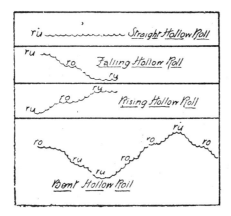

alternately rising and falling, the tour is called bent
Hollow Roll, rorororururururoro, and so on. The
above drawing will make this clear.

Hollow Roll has the widest range of all the rolling tours, and, therefore, it varies considerably in pitch, as also in tone colour. For this reason it is regarded by many as the most beautiful of all the tours. These are matters of taste. It is very difficult to cultivate it deep, and there is always a danger of it going faulty, indefinite, nasal. Straight Hollow Roll, even when deep, is always sung on one note; a good falling roll sounds better, but the ideal is the deep, bent variety, rising and falling in several keys.

Reviser's Note

Schwirre is not now included in the song standard. As a very high pitched Bell roll with a sibilant sound it would be marked as faulty unless it was sung very quietly.

CHAPTER XIV

SIMPLE, DISCONTINUOUS TOURS IN BELL-LIKE FORM

THE characteristic of these tours lies in the fact that the syllables follow one another in a certain unconnected manner, so that there is a pause, a tiny interval, as it were, discernible between each. In

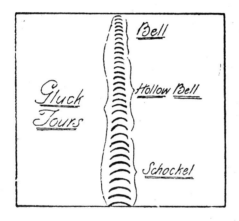

the Roll tours the pause or space is filled up, bridged over, by the intervening " r," whereas in the bell-like tours there is no " r."

To this division of tours belong Bell, the high-toned tour, Hollow Bell, somewhat lower, deep Schockel, Gluck and Flutes.

The ground tone rests on " i," as in Schwirre and

Bell Roll.   The consonants are l, h, d; the syllables formed by combination, therefore, are lilili-hihihi— dididi.

The quality depends upon the fullness and purity of the vowel sound, the force of the consonants, l, h, d, and the measure of the pauses. These pauses regulate the tempo, the beat, in other words the rate at which the syllables are repeated.

THE HAMMERING BELL

Lilili gives the best effect, if not too slow, and the effect is also good with hihihi if the beat be not too slow, otherwise the tour is jerky. Dididi is only good when the " d " is feeble, and the " i " pure and soft; the beat should be fast. If the vowel is hard and the consonant is strongly marked, the tour has a knocking effect, and may be called Hammering Bell.

As its name implies, a good Bell tour reminds one of the sound and the beat of a little tinkling silver bell. The simpler the sound, the more beautiful is the effect. The tour loses value if the vowel " i " is not pure or borders on " e."

Bell is faulty if any but the above-named consonants come in; " s," combined with " d " (dsidsidsi or dsedsedse) is very dangerous; these noisy, unmusical and, therefore, ugly combinations, stifle the ground tone, and this series of syllables leads to Schnetter (dschedschedsche).

Bell is sharp when the " i " is very thin and very high, with " d " or " h " (perhaps a trace of " s ") sung in sharply divided syllables.

Nasal Bell is a melancholy tour on i, e, or a, combined with n and s, ninini sni-sni-sni snesnesne, snäsnäsnä. It is absolutely worthless.

Bell is somewhat undesirable if slow; the identity of the tour gets lost, and the good effect suffers. In this class of tour the beat should be faster in the higher than in the lower pitch; there should be more movement. Slow Bell is wearisome and lacks connectiveness, for the reason that the higher i-sounds lack fullness. With Schockel, on the contrary, a slow movement is very beautiful, because the deep " o " and " u " sounds ring out in full-toned rich volume, thus filling up the larger interval in the heat.

Although Bell is only reckoned as a fair quality tour, it should not be despised, as it makes an agreeable variation in Canary song. In years gone by, one came across some wonderfully pure Bell and this fact proves that, though lightly esteemed in this present day, it is capable of being soundly developed, in spite of its easy degeneration and consequent difficulty in cultivation.

HOLLOW BELL

The ground tone is " ü "; the consonants are l and h (lululu, hühühü); its composition, therefore, is very simple.

The quality depends upon a pure " ü " with a soft " l " or " h." The vowel varies in roundness and fullness, so heightening or lessening the tonality. The l gives the song a delightful lulling lullaby effect, and is a better tour than Hollow Bell with h.

The h lengthens out the syllables so that the structure becomes loose, and the effect is jerky, hammering or dragging, sometimes baying (as a hound), and so we have the tour described as slow, hammering, etc.; nevertheless, if these forms are sung pure, the tour may be classed as fair. Hollow Bell is faulty when the key vowel does not ring true, and borders on e or ä. When nasal, it may be dangerous.

Hollow Bell should come between Bell and Schockel on the register, and in this position it is reckoned as a good tour. Its range is greater, and its tonality better than that of simple Bell, and it should therefore score more on the judging standard.

SCHOCKEL

The ground tones of Schockel are the same as Hollow Roll, deep ü, o, u, also a, ä, ö, e. The consonants are h and l, occasionally g and b, ho-ho-ho, hu-hu-hu, hü-hü-hü, lo-lo-lo, lu-lu-lu, lü-lü-lü, etc., etc.

Schockel cannot be confused with Hollow Roll, for it does not roll; the " r " is entirely absent. The trilling tour Hollow Roll does not ring out its notes in separate beats like Schockel, but pours forth a roll in tremolo form, and, therefore, one should not be mistaken for the other. In Schockel, the purity of the vowel is the measure of the quality; the consonants are of less importance. It is best sung on pure u, o, ü; on a it is not so good, tending, as it does, towards flatness. On ö, e and ä it is apt to degenerate into the nasal. The consonants h and l are, as a rule, only slightly audible, whilst g and b have a somewhat angular beat. Most of the faults in Schockel occur in the vowel section, and incline to nasal.

Bell has been likened to the tinkle of a tiny bell,

Hollow Bell to the sound of a larger, and Schockel to that of a big bell.

Schockel has been described as a long, lowly-drawn-out Hollow Bell tour. A fine exhibition of true, deep Schockel is where the beat is first slow, then quickens, the tone at the same time gaining in volume, a wonderful intensity of fullness; the beats then slow down again and gradually die away.

Schockel is never "bent," because it is a discontinuous tour. The notes of Hollow Roll are strung together in one unbroken (continuous) chain, and, like a chain, may be bent. The notes in Schockel, on the contrary, do not form a run, they consist of a succession of beats separated by tiny pauses or intervals, and therefore can only rise and fall. The diversity in modulation, the change in the variety, which deep Schockel brings in alongside Hollow Roll heighten its value. There is a general desire to hear this tour in our present-day songster, and for that reason it is very much sought after. In conclusion we would say that Schockel is deep sister to Hollow Bell.

GLUCK

In Gluck the best ground tones are u and o, the good are ö and ü, the fair to faulty are a, e, ö, ä, i. The consonants are gl, kl, bl:—Gluk-gluk-gluk, glok-glok-glok, etc. Blukluk-blukluk, bloklokloklok, etc.

In the Gluck tours and their variations the separate (discontinuous) syllables are plainly distinguishable. The tonality in the deeper kinds of Gluck is better in measure as the syllables are more distinctly divided off. If the consonants are brought too closely together, that

F

is to say, if the song is too fast, the ground tone is at times smothered, so that the effect is clattering, spluttering, shallow. If, on the other hand, the ground tone has the predominance, the effect is very charming, especially if it be a pure, deep, full hollow. This we call Hollow Gluck. This variety is also called simple (plain) Gluck.

Bell Gluck, as the name implies, is higher up the scale, and has for ground tone ü with an i accompanying, thus—glüi-glüi-glüi, which gives it a double effect.

In double Gluck there is no "i," as in Bell Gluck. Immediately after the deep accentuated Gluck sound one hears, as it were, a faint echo of Gluck an octave or a fifth higher.

THE PLEASING WATER GLUCK

Another pleasing variety is Water Gluck. It is somewhat similar to the sound caused by a little drop of water falling into water, and the after-drip of the rebounding drop. In a true sense it is also a double Gluck, because you get the deep u-sound with "i," on the after beat.

The consonants bl and gl must be soft (bluik-bluik, gloik-gloik). It differs therefore from Hollow Gluck by its double character and its water effect. When weak and faulty it sounds on a and ä, and the consonants are hard.

By reason of their own peculiar construction, of their extensive variations, and consequent changes in tone effect, the Gluck tours form an important group in the treasure house of the Song Canary. In former years they were cultivated very largely, and with great success,

being both pure and artistic. Being, however, difficult
to breed, and lightly esteemed in consequence, they fell
out of the running, as the Hollow Roll bird, which in the
meantime became " fashionable," was easier to breed
pure, and also easier to sell. There was scant reward,
therefore, for the breeder of Gluck birds. The cultivation of the Gluck tours has again lately set in with
success, and is being made a study of by fanciers, thus
livening up the sporting instinct.

FLUTES

The very good ground tones are u, o, ü. The good
ones are ü, i, au, a. The fair and sometimes faulty are
i, e, ä, ö, iu, iau, io. The best consonant is a soft d,
the next best is t. The bad are ts, tz. Each flute is
composed of one syllable (monosyllable).

A pure vowel with soft a has a good effect; the
deeper and the middle register flutes are of more value
than the higher pitched, because the tone of the former
is better. Anyhow, high flutes must be tender and soft,
in order to escape being faulty. If the pure vowel sound
is lengthened somewhat, it has a drawn-out, melancholy,
plaintive effect; some of these flutes are very beautiful.

The impure vowels, ä, ö, e, give us nasal flutes.
Hard flutes occur with the consonant t (tü); when sung
short many such will be hammering flutes, and they may
be found on all the notes of the register; on the higher
notes they also come out as sharp flutes. Sharp, also, is
the effect if an s or z comes between t and the vowel,
thus :—tsi, tzi, tziau.

The effect in flutes is heightened when the separate

F*

syllables are sung discreetly and in moderation, and loses in value when they are too hasty, ragged, with frequent repetition in one long succession. A good bird should not sing more than four flutes on one note (du-du-du-du). If he changes his key, however, the song is enhanced, and in spite of the length, the effect may be beautiful (du-du-du-dü-dü-dü-do-do).

Flutes belong to the class of simplest tours. Looking upon a bird's tours collectively as one performance, flutes may heighten the general effect, as, for instance, a finish to Schockel and Hollow Bell, or in a transition from Hollow tours into Bass, or when deep, as a prelude to the song.

A PLEASING CHANGE IN SONG

When introduced at the right time in the right place they make a pleasing change in the division of the song, forming a bridge between the Roll tours and the Bell tours, or *vice versa*. On the other hand, many flutes interspersed here and there spoil the song and interfere with the unfolding of the other tours.

As simple, monosyllabic tours, flutes have little importance from a strain-breeding point of view, but, being tours of accompaniment, and seeing that, in spite of their great variety, they must not be too plentiful nor be too conspicuous in any single performance, their possible scoring points should be fairly high on the judging standard. Points should also be reckoned in the general effect column, for or against, according to the manner in which they are introduced and in so far as they spoil or enhance the effect.

CHAPTER XV

COMPOUND TOURS, PARTLY IN ROLLING, PARTLY IN BELL-LIKE FORM

I N these tours we get syllables with a large accumulation of consonants, combined with hollow vowel sounds. Frequently the syllables, taken singly, are rolling in their nature, but in their sequence they are divided off by little pauses or intervals, and therefore are, so to speak, bell-like or Schockel-like (rocking, swinging), and Gluck-like. To this division belong Knorre (bass), Koller, Water Roll, and Gluck Roll.

KNORRE (BASS)

Composition. The best ground tones are o and u; the less valuable are e, a, ä. The consonant in evidence in this tour is r of a double and treble force (rrr) in conjunction with g, k, and n (knorrr, korrr, kurrr, knurrr).

Bass may run its course in a rolling, continuous form; such a tour may be described as Bass Roll. If the cohesion is broken (discontinuous), so that the run is divided up by tiny beats or intervals, and as it were rocking (schockel-like) or gluck-like, then the performance is partaking of the bell-like, ringing character. Diversions of this nature are known as Gluck Bass, Schockel Bass, Koller Bass.

All varieties of Bass must be sung hollow, with the

closed beak, otherwise they are not nice. In Bass Roll
the vowels and consonants should be equally balanced
—*i.e.,* they should be emphasized with the same force;
the result will be a vigorous purring, firmly, evenly,
closely knit together.

What there was of Knorre (Bass Roll sung on the o)
fifteen years ago or so was good. At that time Knorre
(Bass Roll sung on a) was in favour and had good points
awarded, but, being shallow, flat and harsh in tonality
it was of little value.

SONG OF EXCEPTIONAL BEAUTY

On the other hand we have now developed out of
Bass Roll a Hollow Bass of exceptional beauty; the
rumbling consonants are in this tour relegated to the
background, the vowel sound comes out plainer, and
one hears at the same time a further ü or i sounding out
a fourth, a fifth, or an octave higher. One therefore has
to do with a double or two-tone Bass (Knorre). The
effect is very pleasing, well balanced throughout, a very
beautiful harmonious combination.

Another grand example of the Bass type is when
the bird starts with a good Bass Roll, and then, passing
on to a yet deeper Hollow Bass, finishes off by widening
out into Gluck-like form. In such a series three kinds
of Bass are heard; the last-named is Gluck Bass (Gluck-
Knorre), in which one can detect a soft l.

Koller Bass predominates in the deepest hollow; the
Knorre sound (rrr) is intermingled with a hollow o and u
is a Schockel, tremolo form. If the Knorre sound lies
quite in the background, the vowel sounds u or o,
gushing forth in a vibrating, shaking Hollow; we should

describe this as a Kullering Hollow rather than as a Knorre.

Of course, complete harmonious balance between the Knorre and this Gluck Hollow or Koller Hollow is the ideal of a fine Bass. So soon as the bird opens his beak, be it ever so slightly, the tour degenerates, the ground tone becomes thereby shallow and nasal, and the consonants sound sharp and rasping.

Bass is of great importance in Canary song. All breeders are agreed that it is the foundation of the song, the bass voice, and it has an agreeable effect upon the whole performance, which is pleasing to the ear. It is no chance product, but requires careful selection and breeding to cultivate and improve upon. The many consonants in these tours (rrr, etc.) by their nature produce notes that lie deep; they need also to be sung uncommonly fast to ensure good tonality. A high-pitched bass of good tone does not exist.

NO SIMPLE MATTER

For these reasons the cultivation of a deep bass is evidently no simple matter. Knorre is of all present-day Hollow Tours the deepest, and, so far as the author has yet been able to verify, the highest bass lies always about an octave to an octave and a half deeper than the deepest Hollow Roll.

Of late years some wonderful variations have been developed from Knorre, so that it can certainly be regarded as the parent tour of many new forms; it is, therefore, the correct thing to reckon it as a fully-qualified tour for strain breeders. On account of its depth, its wide range of tone, its wonderful capacity for variation, its difficulty in cultivation and its position as a parent or strain tour, it is fully qualified to rank with Hollow Roll in value.

WATER ROLLS

Composition. The good ground tones are based on the vowels o, u, ü; if on a they are less valuable. The accompanying consonants are w, g, d, d, l, r, b, and so arranged that they form syllables, such as the following :—gwudlrudlgwudlrudl; rodlgwodlrudlrodl; gwadlradlgwadradl; bliudlrudlbliudlrudl, bludlrudl-bludlrudl; bliudlriudlriudlbliudl.

The play of the Water Rolls reminds us of the gurgling, rushing, bubbling of a tiny brook, whirling and eddying over its pebbly shallows. We may imitate the sound somewhat by dipping little tubes of various sizes in water and blowing through them. The larger the tube the deeper the tone; the deeper it is dipped into the water the more hollow, subdued and soft is the resultant tone. Now, if the tube be slowly withdrawn, one can plainly detect a weakening of the ground tone and a stronger outflow of air bubbles until, when the surface is reached, the bubbling becomes a weak, broad, splashing ripple which has no value for producing effect.

In the Canary song we make a distinction between a simple Water Roll, which splashes a little more or less, and its deeper sister tours, Hollow Water Roll or Kuller-ing Water Roll, which are more beautiful and valuable. Both these are sung with the beak quite closed, the bl and dl sounds are softly intoned, and, together with the Schockel or swing-like movement, this gives a very charming effect. The best quality tour is sung deep on the vowel u.

These Water Rolls are therefore precious jewels in the storehouse of our songsters, and it is only birds of the deepest strains which are able to perform such without detriment to the other parts of their song.

Water Rolls are of the greatest importance in the furtherance of the development of Canary song; the uncommonly deep pitch is inexhaustible for the production of fresh forms and variations.

Like the Bass tours, they are a fertile source of tone, deep, fundamental, parent tours, and really deserve to stand on a level for points with Hollow Roll and Knorre. In their shallow and weaker forms they may certainly also be quite as dangerous.

KOLLER

The ground tones of Koller are o, u, ü, ö, öi, au, eu. The consonants are bl, gw, kw, r, l. The syllables sung in Koller are brloiroiluilui—brüillüillüi, blöiroirui —blrauiröiloi, gwlräiroirui—kwlreuiliullüi.

Koller may be sung in two styles—namely, as Hollow Koller and Water Koller. The Hollow Koller style gives the impression of relationship with Hollow Roll, the Water Koller style leans towards the Water Roll, Knorre, and Gluck family.

A characteristic of Koller is the " i " sound ringing out in each beat, while alternating deep down we have the sounds u, ö, ü, au, oo, or eu rocked in (schockelled) in combination with the consonants l, h, or rl. The effect produced is a series of syllables, succession of beats, of a two-voiced and three-voiced nature, having somewhat of the effect of a trichord.

One description of the rise and fall of what gives an effect of a three-toned or trichord Koller is given thus:—The " ri " moves on with a roll an octave higher than the deep Koller breast notes, and, like these, it changes its pitch at the same time; in other words, the " ri " rises and falls, while at the same time, in the deeper key, a tremolo lüllüllü, combined with lallalla, rises to lillilli, combined with lüllüllü, to fall deep on to lullo, lollo, bloblloblo, or kollokollo.

In Koller, one hears nothing of Knorre, nothing of Hollow Roll, and nothing of Gluck, but a pure Hollow in quick, rhythmic movement. The bird, in fact, sings the word Koller. As we say Knorre when the bird sings Bass, so we call the tour Koller when a bird sings the text—kollerkollerkoller, etc.

WONDERFUL MUSICAL EFFECTS

Here let us remark that there are variations; sometimes the " k " is left out, and so we have ollerolleroller, another bird will slur over the " r," and one hears kollokollokollo; sometimes the " k " is soft or is replaced by " b "; sometimes in place of the " o " we get " ü " (kuller), or e, ü, a. According as a consonant is left out or another is introduced, the effect differs. We get thus certain variations, which are, however, fundamentally Koller-forms. In those of medium depth one may plainly detect the treble effect, whereas in those of deeper pitch one may hear the double effect.

The wonderful musical effects which Koller produces

constitute a singularly beautiful diversity in Canary song, which is bound to bring delight to every one with good taste and judgment. We know that many years ago, some birds had, besides the above style of Koller, a very deep Hollow Roll, a brilliant Knorre, and no nasty faults, not even Aufzug; they sang so fluently, fervently, and with such modulation that it was astonishing. It has therefore been established that Koller birds can be bred pure both as to tours and quality of tone, so that those breeders who are afraid of cultivating Koller on account of its presumed liability to produce faults are in the wrong.

On account of its wonderful effect, its many-sidedness, its difficulty to breed, and its importance as being a deep, fundamental tour, Koller is highly esteemed. In past times it was called the " Queen of all the Tours." During the period devoted to breeding the easier Hollow Roll it seldom appeared, but of late endeavours have happily been made to resuscitate this deep tour and to widen its popularity, and thereby to further enrich the bird's noble song. Whether we succeed in winning back the early style of Koller time alone will show. Koller is at present valued for points the same as Hollow Roll and Bass Roll.

GLUCK ROLLS

The good ground tours in Gluck Rolls are u, o, u; the less valued are e, a, ä. The consonants are g, k, r, l. The syllables formed are glruk-glruk-gluk, glrok-glrok-glrok, glrük-glrük-glrük.

Gluck and Roll being here combined, the result is a discontinuous Roll tour. Each syllable possesses an " r," which gives it the roll form; each syllable, however, is separated by a tiny interval, so that one detects a succession of rolling syllables separated in a scarcely perceptible manner by a series of beats. As we have here the consonant " g," the beats are plainly discernible.

Like all other tours, the quality (tonality) depends upon the purity and fullness of the ground tones, the softness of the consonants, and the knitting together of the syllables; in other words, the perfection of the run. Impure, faulty vowels sound nasal, loud consonants sound hard and pointed; a slack run leaves the tours loose, clattering, watery, which is also bad. To perform the tour well so that the bird produces a full tone, in spite of the numerous swift beats, he needs strong lung force. The finest form of this tour is Hollow Gluck Roll.

Gluck Rolls are plentiful; when deep, they are fine passages, and therefore enrich the song. Already the deep position of this tour is commanding higher appreciation, for all deep tours should—nay, must—be fostered.

Reviser's Note

The current song standard draws a distinction between Water Roll and Deep Bubbling water tour. In Deep Bubble the sound like bubbles bursting is superimposed on the underlying rippling water sound

As mentioned in previous chapters these water tours are dangerous to breed for, due to the tendency for the water sound to spread into the Hollow tours with adverse effects on their tonality. Deep Bubbling Water Tour is almost extinct in contemporary birds and is seldom heard.

Koller has been extinct for many years and is not part of the repertoire of modern Rollers.

CHAPTER XVI

FAULTS IN SONG

FAULTY tours are those which come short of the purity and tonality required. Examples of faulty delivery exist in every tour, and these, of course, lower or entirely annul their value. The tours we have named have faults, which we here enumerate :—

Hollow Roll.—Nasal, broad, watery, scratchy, dull, thin.

Bass.—Nasal, broad, jarring, watery, rattling, crackling, weak.

Koller.—Nasal, loose, weak.

Schockel.—Nasal.

Hollow Bell.—Nasal, jumpy, dragging, baying, hard.

Gluck.—Nasal, blunt, weak, clattering, loud.

Water Roll.—Nasal, broad, hard, sharp.

Bell.—Nasal, jerky, hammering, sharp, thin, shrill, penetrating, dragging, schnetter-like.

Bell Roll.—Nasal, hard, broad, weak, sharp.

Schwirre.—Nasal, sharp, hard, broad, weak, shrill, thin, schnetter-like.

Flutes.—Nasal, hard, sharp, hammering, penetrating, thin.

Besides valuable tours with faults as above, there are others which we might also describe as bad tours and very dangerous to song. They are :—(1) Aufzug, (2) call notes, interjections, (3) Zitt, Schnetter, Schnatter, Chop.

Aufzug (short breath, recovery).—The ground tones of Aufzug are i, e, ä, ö, ie. The consonants are tz, trs, ck, g, d, st. The syllables formed are tzri, strisz, gritz, ritsch, ritz, retsch.

We get several qualities, soft, quiet, long, short, weak, hard, shrill and sharp. Among other things the consonants are sharply accentuated in combination with the vowels given and the beak is opened wide. Where the Aufzug is weak, the opening of the beak is not so pronounced. Points are deducted according to the extent of the demerits.

INTERJECTIONS AND EXCLAMATIONS

By call notes we understand so-called interjections and exclamations with which some birds prelude their song or introduce into it during its course. In present-day birds they have happily become scarce, art and diligence having succeeded in breeding them out; for all that there are faulty specimens occasionally to be met with. The sounds we come across are wid-wid, id-id, wis-wis (whispering), will-will, tzick-tzick, tzitt-tzitt, siss-siss-siss, tzep-tzep, hie, eye, wy, and similar objectionable noises. The penalty points for these range higher comparatively than in Aufzug.

Tzitt, Schnetter, Schnatter.—These three bad faults are also no longer so plentiful as in former times. The Tzitt fault occurs when it appears no longer as the interjection already referred to, but is repeated continuously as a tour. Schnetter proceeds from a weak, unmusical, hard or broad Schwirre or Bell, and also in the form of dsched-sched-sche. Schnatter is related to Schnetter, harping on dschad-dschad, and is the stepping-stone to the Chopping noise (Chop), tzschepp, tzschapp, tzschiapp. In Schnatter and Chop the lower mandible is freely worked up and down. Needless to say, these can earn no points; they have no value whatever, and birds possessing them are not to be recommended for the breeding-room.

LEADING QUALITIES

In valuing the tours singly as integral parts of the whole, certain leading qualities should be borne in mind.

1.—The position of the tour on the register—*i.e.,* its musical pitch, high, medium, low, etc.

2.—Purity (not nasal, etc.).

3.—Tonality (the finish, the harmonious ring of the tour).

4.—Fullness (not broad, thin, weak).

5.—Force (well defined, distinct, not feeble, etc.).

6.—Length (duration).

Besides these six qualities other things have to be taken into account when we view the song as a whole—namely, the manner and way in which the tours hang together, their progression and connection, their sequence, their style of variation, repetition of the same tour in the song, the number of tours of first category, the harmonious and inharmonious tours, the structure of the song, and its effect upon a well-trained sympathetic, musical ear, also the harmonious assembling of the second and third category tours into one whole, well-knit, self-contained song.

The above outlines the requirements which have to be met in order to make a good harmonious execution and delivery. On the competition judging-sheets, the words " General effect " are used to express their harmonious delivery, and points are given according to its excellence, just as they are given to each individual tour.

Reviser's Note

Bell Gluck is now listed amongst the faults in The Roller's song and birds singing it are penalised at the contests. In the descriptions of Hollow bell and Schockel the difference in style of delivery could be emphasised a little more. In Schockel the notes are completely separate and aspirated, whereas in Hollow bell they are to some extent linked by the characteristic semi-vowel "L" sound.

CHAPTER XVII

THE BELL TOURS

THE name "Hollow Bell," as given to one of the tours of the Roller Canary, speaks for itself; it is a bell tour with a hollow sound. The border limit between bell and hollow bell can scarcely be described in words; it is a difference which the breeder must himself discover. As a rule it should not be a difficult matter to a well-attuned ear to apprehend the difference between the two. In the first place, Hollow Bell is pitched deeper than Bell, and the ground tone is a full sounding ü (the French u), and sometimes " ou," while the Bell Tour simple is sounded on " ee."

HOW BIRD-SONG IS PRODUCED

If we examine the difference in our own mode of delivery, we find that, on pronouncing this syllable " ee," the sound is a shallow one, whereas to pronounce the French u (ü) the mouth widens and arches somewhat; in other words, hollows itself. The tongue also is set further back, and thus widens the space round the palate, and, in consequence, the ü sounds fuller, rounder, more hollow than the ee.

In a similar fashion, the variations of tone are produced in the bird's throat; his vocal chords produce the ground note, and in the " hollowing " of his throat and beak are the secrets of its fullness and tonality.

THE PRODUCTION OF BIRD SONG.

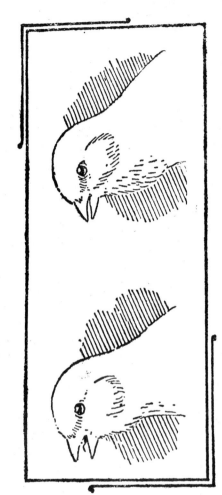

Bird Singing Bell.   Bird Singing Hollow Bell.

In bell we always have the opened beak; in hollow bell, the beak is closed, or, at any rate, only very slightly open, the beak and throat space is hollowed out, and this means that the " ü " gains in volume and comes out as a full, round, hollow tour. The closer the beak is kept the more perfect the sound.

The finest effect and the fullest tonality in this tour are produced when the bird, with closed beak, sounds a full " ü " with a gently breathed consonant " l," thus: " lüllüllüllü "; hollow bell, with the " h," thus: " Hühühühü," is not commonly met with, but is not exactly a bad form.

ON VALUING A TOUR

The speed at which the syllables follow one another, the rate of delivery, is a point for consideration in valuing the tour as well as its tone quality; a vigorous delivery, with fast repetition of the syllables well connected together, is not tiresome, and will have scarcely any prejudicial effect on the tunefulness of the song, but a slow, dragging, tame delivery is wearisome and blunts the effect, the song losing thereby all freshness and animation.

In this latter instance we have an example of so-called dragging Hollow Bell, which is not worth much. It is common to hear this tour opening out in correct time and then for a moment slowing down slightly in the middle of the delivery soon to launch out again fresh and free. This is a very agreeable variation, the effect being very pleasing.

Hollow Bell, as also the Bell tour, may start with the consonant " r," being quickly changed to the characteristic " l "—" rüllüllüllü.". One often comes across the expression, " Bent hollow bell," but bell tours are not bent, for between the syllables given above there are tiny, but distinct, intervals which are a characteristic of these tours.

What, on the other hand, can be bent? The reply is, only a cohesive structure. One can bend a cane, but one cannot speak so of a chain. Rolling tours may bend, but not bell tours. As a matter of fact, however, when we have falling or rising hollow bell we get bending, curving tone effects; these are transitions with a roll.

Of all the tours hollow bell suffers the least from faulty variation; it is not an exceptional work of art, and is to be found in most strains. One fault to avoid is nasal hollow bell; its ground tones are " a " and " ee," with the beak open.

GOOD AND BAD SCHOCKEL

Schockel is brother to Hollow Bell, and is often dubbed Hollow Schockel, but this is just as superfluous as calling coal black. I should define Schockel as deep tones rocking, waving, swinging, and shaking with the rhythm of a bell. The ground notes are " ü," " o," " ou," and the consonants are " l " or " h "—" lüllül," " hoho," " houhou."

Schockel, in conjunction with deep, hollow roll, now rising, now falling, is a prime tour when clear and pure and well defined. There is something about this tour which gives it its value and ennobles it as one of the masterpieces in song; it is its sympathetic, melancholy softness. There is a mysterious tragic note running through it.

Schockel belongs to the category of Bell tours; in fact, it is a deep hollow bell. Many breeders confuse it with the medium-pitched hollow bell, which also has a Schockel-like (rocking) effect, but this not true Schockel; it lacks the deep, soul-stirring melody.

Schockel has its faulty variations. In consequence of its depth and its full structure, it creates a strong demand on the bird's song apparatus, and if this lacks the required amount of strength and vigour to produce the depth of tone we may get Schockel that is weak, thin, or nasal. We sometimes hear men speak of laughing Schockel, which, however, is a degenerated variety, the ground note being " a."

Schockel must not be confounded with the tremolo roll tours. In the latter we have rolling, quivering, trilling tones; in the former, we have an articulation backwards and forwards, a swinging, waving movement of the song syllables. Here we would repeat the old illustration—namely, Bell, Hollow Bell, and Schockel represent three bells, a small tinkling bell, a medium-sized one, and a deep-toned bell. To correct any doubt as to what is a bell tour and what is a roll, it might help to keep the following adage in mind : " what rings does not roll, and that which rolls does not ring."

CHAPTER XVIII

THE JUDGING OF ROLLERS

FAULTS OF OMISSION AND FAULTS OF COMMISSION IN COMPETITION

This Chapter on Judging was contributed by the well-known Judge, the late M . H. G. Hill.

WHAT do we mean when we say " Faults?" We have tried to catalogue them, but have we succeeded in doing so? My own experience has taught me that some of those birds which, judged by that catalogue as faulty, are far better songsters than many which are ticketed as " pure."

I will endeavour to explain why I hold that view, in the hope that beginners in the Fancy will be guided thereby to think for themselves, and not be imprisoned by hard and fast catalogue rules.

The cataloguing of faults is useful as a guide, but it does not, and cannot, embrace all that should be considered as faulty in a Roller's song, and its great drawback is that it often places a ban on some fault that is in the catalogue, whilst blinding us to a more serious fault that is not in that penalty list, and so escapes the visible sign of penalization.

As an illustration, I have often heard novices regard a bird with horror because he has in his song aufzug, rather sharp flutes, or a bell that is delivered rather

vigorously, even though it be in the correct register for
that tour, and those same novices have looked on another
bird as a faultless singer—a bird that, owing to the faulty
habit of his song, or his thin and " reedy " tone, I would
not have at any price.

This because the one fault is catalogued for him to
read, and the other, and more dangerous one, is not.
The latter fault is penalized by every good judge, though
it is not in the list of catalogued faults; it is penalized by
allowing less for general effect. But the novice often
does not know that, so is apt to be led astray.

THE DEFINITION OF FAULTS

What, then, is our definition of " faults "? There
are faults of omission as well as commission. But to
avoid confusion, we will define " fault " as something
in the bird's song which offends the ear of a good judge
as being opposed to the ideal.

We all know what sharp bell, sharp flutes and aufzug
are, to take the more common of the catalogued faults.
Let us deal with the faults which are not catalogued
and therefore not so familiar to the eye, even though
they be offensive to the trained ear.

First, there is the bird which gives up eighty per
cent. of his song period to the cheap, or low-scoring
tours, only touching at intervals the deeper and more
classical tours.

Every man who has judged Rollers knows what I
mean. You hear a bird again and again go over that
cheap stuff, and at last, when patience is nearly ex-
hausted, he will take a fit and drop down to something

of merit. That is a faulty bird, even though he may
not possess one of the catalogued faults. I will compare
with him a bird who hangs on well to his deep tours,
only very slightly touching the cheap ones; a bird that
pleases you and holds your ear, but occasionally brings
one of the catalogued faults, not very badly, but sufficient
to gain him a black mark.

" BANG   GOES   SAXPENCE "

" Here," says the novice, looking at his catalogue,
" is a faulty bird—and here's another that's pure, never
a penalized point!" And "bang goes saxpence," or a
little more, on the faultless singer.

That novice is going wrong. The one bird, a grand
singer, has one little fault of commission, the other a
serious fault of omission. The one does his work well
and makes a little slip, the other does his work badly and
makes a fed-up judge. The one may breed you and train
you a champion, the other will give you nothing much
better than himself, for if there is one thing above all
others that young Rollers imitate in the tutor, it is this
lazy habit of sticking to the cheap and easy tours.

Let us compare now this good, deep, fine-toned
singer with one little fault with other types of songsters
deemed faultless because they have no fault that is in
the catalogue of faults.

Take the bird of thin and reedy tone, beside the
other bird as a tin whistle to an oboe. He has a nice
range of tours, perhaps, according to paper. He sings
no aufzug or sharp flute or sharp bell. He passed
without a mark against him.

But his song is a reedy murmur, with no music in

it—no " guts," to use an expressive term. There are some who will tell you he is a " soft " bird, whereas he simply lacks power, volume, tone. As a matter of fact, he is not in the same street with the bird mentioned above with the mark against him, either as a contest bird, a tutor or a sire.

A WRONG IDEA OF MODERN TIMES

It is for this reason that I have always opposed the idea that no bird with a mark against him should ever win a first or any other prize, when there are these " pure " (so-called) singers in the same class.

Having expressed these views, I must hasten to add important qualifications. It must not be understood that I hold a brief for sharp bell, sharp flutes and aufzug—I do not. Nor do I think that any bird penalized for two faults should ever be a first prize-winner. There is a vast difference between two and one. The law, you know, gives every dog first bite—but he mustn't take another, or off goes his head.

My firm conviction is that a really high-class bird with one fault is still a good bird, and that a second-rate bird, with no fault, is still a second-rater. All things being equal, and the scores level, the unpenalized bird should win, and that has always been done. But no more than that if we value the progress of the birds.

When we hear it said, then, that all winners in champion classes ought to be " pure " birds, let us think of our definition, remember how many faults there are that have no penalty column, and how few of those so-called " pure " birds are really free from even more serious faults than the bird penalized has himself.

FAULTS IN DEGREE

Now we will consider faults in degree, as we have considered them in kind. What is the degree of fault than can be forgiven, or when penalized, should not count against a bird winning?

That is difficult to express by any rule of thumb. It depends solely on the construction of the bird's song, the tone of the song throughout and the frequency with which the fault enters that song. It can be decided on the judging-table and there alone.

It depends chiefly on the extent to which the fault jars on the ear. A bird that just touches sharp bell, and then immediately, almost before your ear has caught it, rolls away on to his deep song again, possesses a fault that, in a full-toned and deep bird, will often add piquancy to his song. The same with a not-too-hard aufzug, gone almost before it is there. In another bird exactly the same degree of fault, followed by his thin, light and toneless song, might jar terribly.

The same with nasal. A rich-toned, full-sounding singer may touch nasal on some of his tours, and it will be not at all displeasing, whilst a weedy-toned bird, on the nasal, makes you want to catch a train. You can only tell what degree of discord there is when you hear the harmony running with it. It is the whole song combined that tells you what the fault is like, and that alone.

Now, as to faults in a tutor. For two years I trained with a bird that had the very worst aufzug in England, and in some of his sons it came out nearly as bad, but in others there was no aufzug at all. I am bound to say that very few of your young will escape sharp bell if it is in the tutor. It is the same with sharp flutes, but they do not always—far from it—bring them as badly as they may be in the tutor.

THEY DO NOT ALWAYS FOLLOW THEIR TUTOR

If you train with a bird that has perfect bell, or even no bell at all, you will find a big proportion of the young come out with sharp bell; and though your tutor may have perfect, or nearly perfect, flutes, some of the young will take them higher and sharper. I have proved again and again that if you train with a bird that sings no bell tour, though the young will develop bell, sharp sometimes, in the training, they will gradually drop it when their song matures, because not hearing the tutor follow them, as it were, they begin to follow him. I have found the same thing apply to sharp flutes, when developed in the young, and no sharp flutes in the tutor bird.

As so many youngsters develop faults even if the tutor does not possess them, is it worth while to put down your champion because he has one fault in his song? For though the pupils may copy his fault, more or less, they will also copy his virtues; and if you use instead that second-rater, passed as " pure," you may find yourself still with the fault and lacking the virtues at the same time.

The most successful breeder of Rollers in this country once said to me :—" What I look for in a tutor are variety, depth, power of tone, and one little fault I never mind." After some years' experience, I don't think I can give the Roller novices any better advice.

FAULTLESS BIRDS NOT ALWAYS THE BEST

If a man has the good luck to possess a champion that has no fault, then he doesn't need advice from any man to use him. But either in contest, breeding-room or training-room I would never put back a good bird just because he had one fault in an otherwise grand song, and put over him a bird not so good, even though the latter did not commit a fault which could be penalized.

It would mean putting many a real champion with one fault into a back seat and hoisting up into premier place third-rate birds whose faults don't happen to come into the catalogued list where the judge puts down a straight stroke, often with a sigh. He has to let the inferior bird go free, except that he sees he doesn't get many for his general effect.

It may be said that these faultless (so-called) birds are bound to be good, for, as well as being unpenalized, they reach their thirty points or so. But that is not the case. A judge has to put down the value of the individual tours when they are sung, however badly those tours are connected, however infrequently the deep tours are heard.

The scores of a bird are only a rough guide to his value. You cannot put down on paper all that goes to make your champion on the judging-table. His habit of song, his organ-like volume of tone, his steady habit of dwelling on the difficult and hard tours, his contemptuous touching of the lighter tours as something unworthy of him—you cannot put down on paper all those virtues in him that make you wish he was yours, any more than you can put down all those uncatalogued faults in the other bird that make you glad you don't possess him.

But I'll tell you what you can do, and it's what I always do. Whatever the scores for the individual tours, I see that it is my best bird that comes out on top. Here the "general effect" column comes in, and I am very glad to see many judges making a larger use of that column than has ever been made before.

But what would be the use of all these efforts on the part of a judge to weigh up everything for and against a bird, those good points which are not catalogued as such, and those faults which are unnamed, if he had to put down into the cards his best bird because he had a penalty mark against him? It would, in my opinion, be the end of all good judging, and, in time, might well make for the end of all good birds.

CONCLUSION

This chapter distills the very essence of what makes a good Roller canary. It should be read again and again until the message is clearly understood. Fortunately not too many birds are bred today which are severely faulty, although of course there will always be some, but many birds still suffer from the uncatalogued faults which are described, and it is important to recognise them for what they are. Throughout the book the importance of depth and purity of tone has been emphasised and the successful fanciers of today, as in years gone by, are those who have learned this lesson well.